Words from The Woods: 2009-2011

Whitey Lueck

Cover photo: The white that one sees in this photo of a wintertime forest of Douglas-firs and bigleaf maples—on Spencer Butte in Eugene, Oregon—is neither snow nor ice. It's *rime-frost* that formed overnight as fog blew past the below-freezing trunks and twigs and lichens and mosses.

Photo taken by the author.

ISBN: 1537321641
ISBN-13: 978-1537321646

HIC ET NUNC

Meaning "here and now" in Latin—and pronounced *hick-ett-nunk*—this is Whitey's mantra when in the woods, to keep his mind focused on where he *is*, instead of where he is *not*. After all, what right does he have to be in the woods, if his mind is in the city?

CONTENTS

ACKNOWLEDGMENT

I am deeply grateful to the McKenzie River Ranger District of the Willamette National Forest, the source of much of the inspiration for the essays that follow.

PREFACE

I suspect that it's been a while since you, dear reader, have read a book's preface that was written by candlelight. But you're reading one now! And it's not because the author is an ascetic who shuns convenience and eschews light bulbs. Rather, it's dark outside, I'm inside my tent, and the nearest electric line is more than a mile away.

Words from "the woods." That's for sure. Virtually every word in this volume was written in the woods. Most of the essays were written in the Douglas-fir forests of Oregon's West Cascades—where I am right now—but a few first appeared on paper while I was visiting the Sitka spruce forests of the central Oregon coast north of Florence.

I'm outside year-round, so I write in all kinds of weather, except when it's just too cold for my fingers to work—but days like that are rare here in Western Oregon. Most of the time, I'm sitting with my back against a tree, or atop a moss-covered bluff with a view out to a distant tree-covered ridge. Or I'm seated cross-legged in the shade of a madrone. When it's wet, I'm under my little lean-to which I fashion by tying a rope a few feet off the ground between two tree trunks and then placing a six-foot by eight-foot green tarp over the rope. Half of the tarp forms the nearly vertical "rear wall" of the lean-to, and the other half the barely sloping "front porch roof" under which I sit, typically atop a day-nest—which you'll read about in one of the essays—of fir or hemlock boughs.

I try to camp out once a month year-round for a stretch of at least three days and two nights. In summer, that gives me a couple of hours each night for writing, if I so choose, after sunset. And in the winter, I spend of course much more time inside my tent—even during the daytime if it's wet weather. But there are also many winter days when, thanks to clear skies and temperature inversions, I'm able to bask very comfortably in the sunshine while sometimes wearing almost nothing at all. (You'll read about *that* in the book's very first essay.)

So you see, the title of this book couldn't be more appropriate. When I'm writing, I'm invariably in *The Woods;* I'm leaning against *trees;* I'm looking out at *trees;* I'm in the shade of a *tree;* and I'm writing on paper made from *trees!*

And where do my ideas for essays come from? Seldom does a week go by that I don't come up with another idea or two or five, most of which never see the light of day, or I'd not get anything else done. Although I wrote more than fifty essays—that eventually became the book *Staying Put in Lane County*—during my year of "confinement" in Lane County, Oregon, in 2014, a typical annual average is more like fifteen to twenty. "Enough," but not a production-line approach that could well take the fun out of the writing.

From first idea to actual writing can be just a matter of minutes. I experience something in the woods, or even occasionally in an urban setting, and I sit down shortly afterward and write about it. It's not hard. Most of the essays flow onto the page almost effortlessly. I'm not boasting; that's just the way it is. I've written for many, many years—including a daily journal since 1973—so I've had lots of practice.

Sometimes, however, years elapse between the time I think of writing about something, and the day when I actually sit down and do it. I never stare at a blank page and wonder, "How do I start?" I wait until I know in my head what I want to say, and only then do I pick up my pencil. One of the essays that sat for years on a "back burner" was included in my previous collection (*Words from the Woods: 2004-2008*). It recalled a very touching event that took place when I lived in western France. I knew I wanted to write about what happened that day, but my emotions always got in the way, shall we say. (The story still makes me sniffle when I re-read it.) But one sunny afternoon, while wandering alone and off-trail in a remote valley along the central Oregon coast, I suddenly felt the urge to write about it. Right then! So I sat down in the moss at the base of an alder tree next to the little creek, and out came the essay—except for some minor editing later—in less than an hour.

Now that you probably know much more than you ever wanted to about the mechanics of my essay writing, and without further ado, it's time to turn the page and delve into these slices of my little life here on what I have referred to more than once as "my favorite planet in the solar system."

Whitey Lueck
In *The Woods* (candle burning)
8 September 2016

THE ART OF BASKING

IT'S JUST AFTER NOON on the day before Christmas, and I'm enjoying life here in the West Cascades of Oregon. The ground is carpeted with about two inches of fresh snow, the temperature is in the mid-30s, and the sun is shining brilliantly in a cloudless sky. And here I sit, wearing nothing but my glasses.

"He must be crazy!" you say. On the contrary, I am confident that all my intellectual faculties are functioning at peak capacity at the moment. You see, I have learned the art of basking, and I am practicing it as I write.

For some curious reason, basking is very little known in our culture. Oh, sure, in the summertime when it's hot out, people lie in the sun because it feels good—or they're trying to get a "tan," which many people consider attractive and a sign of good health. And in the wintertime, in areas where winter sports are popular, one sometimes sees skiers or skaters—when sitting down and taking a break—with their faces pointed skyward on sunny days. They're clearly "soaking up the sun," but in my view they're only Beginner Baskers, because they usually still have most of their clothes on. And how can one efficiently warm one's body with sunshine if it is covered with multiple layers of clothing?

My first exposure (so to speak) to basking was when I was living in northern Sweden in the mid-1970s. Year-round, the sun is seldom very strong at that latitude—nor the air temperature very warm—and people take every opportunity to soak up as much sun over as much of their body as possible. In the downtown pedestrian mall in Umeå, the small city closest to where I lived, there were long rows of benches that all faced due south. On sunny days at almost any time of year, I could find there several to a dozen or more people sitting quietly on the benches and facing the sun. (In that setting, however, the baskers were always fully clothed.)

My first experience with "domestic" basking—back in the U.S.—was in Madison, Wisconsin, where I went to graduate school. Many winter days were wonderfully sunny, and I soon found a couple of excellent spots on campus where, after swimming laps mid-day at the university pool, I would eat my picnic lunch and just bask for a while before heading back to classes or to my office. Even when the snow was deep and a frigid wind was blowing from the northwest, the dark red brick wall on the south side of the Steenbock Science Library building was out of the wind, warm, and inviting. (Interestingly, however, I was apparently the only person ever to take advantage of the wall's generous invitation.)

Since moving back to western Oregon in 1983 and establishing my tradition of frequent trips to the West Cascades, I have perfected the art of basking. Although western Oregon weather from June through October is mostly sunny, we can suffer during the winter months from sun deprivation, especially in the southern Willamette Valley which is socked in with fog for many days every winter. But when it's foggy in Eugene, the sun is almost always shining everywhere else, so I happily hop the bus to the Cascades—as I did earlier today—to spend a few hours blissfully basking.

The principles of professional basking are few:

- You need to take your clothes off—or strip to the waist anyway, or at the *very* least roll up your sleeves and pull up your shirt to expose your midriff—so the sun can reach your body to both warm you and make a little vitamin D.

- You must find a spot that is out of the wind and faces south. In urban areas, the best places are stone or brick walls—the darker the color, the better. (The uppermost level of a parking garage is, in my experience, ideal for both maximum sun exposure and for privacy—but watch out for those pesky security cameras.) In the wilds, the best places are south-facing slopes or cliffs, preferably in a concave area or depression, or at the base of evergreen shrubs or a large tree trunk—where there will be the least wind and the sun's rays will be most focused.

- You need to be able to lie on the ground atop an insulated pad or an article of clothing; or, if you're sitting up, have your back against a wall, cliff, or tree trunk. This keeps the shady side of your body from getting cold. If you can't do that, you'll need to at least drape a sweater or coat over your shoulders and back—while exposing your naked front side to the full sun.

- Your body—or the part(s) you want warmed—needs to be as perpendicular to the sun's rays as possible, for maximum effect.

- From November through January, when the sun is lowest, the best basking hours are from 10 a.m. until 2 or 3 p.m. But especially well-chosen basking sites can warm you already quite early in the morning and late into the afternoon; seek out such spots and tell no one else about them.

I don't anticipate that publicizing my "basking secrets" here is going to create much competition for my favorite spots. But it would be great to sometime encounter someone else doing what comes so naturally to most other animals, but among humans seems to be an almost forgotten practice. See you out in the sunshine some winter day!

MY VERY FIRST ESSAY:
THE INCIDENT AT MADRONE BLUFF

AS MANY PEOPLE KNOW, I have a special spot in the Cascade Mountains where I go at least once or twice a month just to be alone. Usually, I take the morning bus up into the mountains, spend the entire day there, then return on the evening bus. It's about 65 miles from my house and costs [*the year this essay was written*] only a 65-cent token one-way. From the end of the line at the McKenzie River Ranger Station of the Willamette National Forest, it's about three miles to my spot, which I reach in part by walking along logging roads, but for the last half-mile or so I go cross-country through the forest. Occasionally, I take along a full backpack and spend a couple of nights camped on the bluff, with day hikes from that base camp, which brings me to my story.

I left Eugene Wednesday morning, 7 October, to spend four days in the mountains as part of my October vacation. The hike into the forest was not unusual. Although it was deer hunting season, I neither encountered nor heard anyone or any shots all day long, and I set up my camp among the red-barked madrone trees and enjoyed a lovely dinner there atop the bluff—aptly named by me Madrone Bluff, for the pink-barked, broadleafed, evergreen trees that grow there—while gazing out across Horse Creek canyon to Olallie Ridge on the opposite side of the valley. A nearly full moon kept my camp illuminated all night long, and I slept a delightful ten hours.

Breakfast was leisurely and, as always, afforded a grand view, framed by the madrones, out across the pristine, wooded valley below. Afterward, I descended to Bull Elk Creek, west of camp, just five minutes away and down a very steep, mossy slope through a dark forest of conifers. There, I filled my water bottles in preparation for the day's hike. Back at camp, I packed my lunch and snacks for the day, closed the tent up tightly in case of a shower, stowed my red Kelty backpack upright under a young Douglas-fir, and hoisted my food stash high into one of the madrone trees out of reach of any animals that might pass through the area during my absence.

When all was in order, I headed east, more or less along the contour, through a magnificent stand of 250-year-old incense-cedars and Douglas-firs, then angled downslope until I reached Horse Creek about a mile away. By then, the thin morning clouds were dissipating and brilliant sunshine was streaming into the valley. I enjoyed my mid-morning snack near the creek, where I leaned against the broadly buttressed trunk of an old redcedar. The rest of the morning, I meandered farther upstream along a broad glacial terrace, in a lush forest of 450-year-old Douglas-firs and redcedars festooned with mosses and carpeted with swordferns and Oregon oxalis. The trunk of one fir was more than eight feet in diameter, by far the largest one I've ever come across in the area.

After a couple of hours of exploring, I was ready for another snack, so I crossed back to the north side of the creek and found a nice sunny spot where I stripped and dove in for a quick swim (water temperature 47 degrees) to get rid of the sweat and grime of the day's exertions. I then relaxed and snacked in the sunshine while reading the chapter of John Muir's *The Mountains of California* about the water ouzel, or dipper, one of which was feeding nearby on aquatic insects and being its cheerful self, singing merrily between dips in the water. The bird appeared to be completely at ease sharing that portion of the stream with a naked blond hominid.

Late afternoon, I headed back along the terrace on the north bank. The going was easy, as I followed a well-traveled elk trail. I then ascended along Bull Elk Creek toward my camp, stopping midway to relax in a mossy glade and recall the day's many delights before tackling the last steep pitch up to Madrone Bluff. As I approached the top, I was grinning over a day well-spent and looking forward to a nice sunset supper. But when I clambered over the last moss-covered boulder and reached the top of the bluff, anticipating the sight of my tidy little camp, I was stupefied to see *nothing*. My camp was gone!

Initially, I thought a passing deer hunter had come upon my camp, and either stolen my equipment, or perhaps playfully hidden it somewhere nearby. But after a few more steps forward and away from the top of the bluff, I caught sight of the remains of my tent, flat as a pancake. My red backpack, however, was nowhere to be seen. And the food stash high in the madrone tree was gone, as well. The overview of the whole site took but a few seconds, and was followed immediately by the realization that my camp had been visited during my absence, not by a hunter, but by a black bear. Indeed, as I rummaged in disbelief through the remains of my gear, I found plenty of evidence: tooth marks on the plastic salt canister and now-empty plastic egg container; claw marks on my sleeping pad; bear slobber and miscellaneous rips and tears on the backpack which had been dragged from the main camp a ways, then abandoned. The only food that was not eaten was the honey (!) which I had in a small glass jar with a metal lid. But the lid had a tooth dent in it and the jar's bottom had a big chip of glass missing, so the bear had at least *tried* to get into it. Oh, and the bear also left me my two oranges that were crushed, but not consumed, as the acidic fruit apparently had not agreed with the bear.

With only an hour before dark, I had to hurry to get things packed up and cover the three miles back to the ranger station. I rolled up the tattered remains of my tent and other gear and more or less made up my backpack, all the while nervously glancing over my shoulder every fifteen or twenty seconds for The Bear, if indeed it was still in the vicinity. I broke camp in record time and headed back down to Bull Elk Creek, then up the other side, my feet moving so fast they must have been just a blur. The adrenalin was really pumping, and the salty sweat from my brow was so profuse that it was pouring into my eyes and burning them. When I finally reached the nearest logging road, I breathed a sigh of relief, took a big swig of water and washed my face with some of the water, then ate a couple of cookies—that I'd carried with me all day in my daypack, so they had been spared—and headed back down to the McKenzie Highway as fast as my already-tired legs could carry me.

Outside the ranger station, which was by then closed, I stashed my backpack, then ran across the highway and down to the river for a quick dip. An absolutely gorgeous orange sky downriver to the west was framed by the tall firs lining both river banks. I ripped off my sweat-drenched clothes and dove in. While I dried off on the mossy bank, I noticed—first with my nose and then with my eyes—a rotting chinook salmon carcass just ten feet away. It's spawning season now here in the Northwest, and the three-foot-long fish had already spawned and died. After putting on fresh, clean clothes, I climbed back up the bank into the narrow strip of forest, then crossed the highway in time to make some semblance of a "supper" from what little food I had left. And, as the nearly full moon rose higher over the nearby forest, I happily boarded the 7:25 p.m. bus back to town.

By 10 p.m., I was back home, full of tales to tell and with no desire at all to go to sleep. I finally got into bed just after midnight and, despite the continuing effect of my adrenalin at keeping my mind awake, my body was so fatigued from the long day that I was soon sound asleep.

(This essay was written on 8 October 1992, the day after "the incident," and was then revised slightly in June 2011.)

WATCHING ROCKS DRY

THERE ARE SOME THINGS IN LIFE that really don't matter much. And there are other things that truly merit close attention and consideration. At the moment, I am attending to one of the latter.

Last night was clear here on the central Oregon coast and a substantial dew developed in open areas such as meadows. But under the forest canopy of Sitka spruces—where my tent is, just south of Strawberry Hill—everything was dry because the spruces collected the dew before it could reach my tent.

After getting out of my sleeping bag, and then out of my tent, I stepped to the edge of the nearby sandy bluff and said good morning to Te Moana Nui A Kiwa—The Great Sea of Kiwa to Polynesians, and what we call the Pacific Ocean—then packed up and headed through the woods toward Gwynn Knoll and Bob Creek. As soon as I came out of the forest, everything was wet with dew, so I kept to the highway shoulder instead of wandering through the meadows south of Bob Creek. Soon, I passed precipitous Bray Point, where the incoming tide was crashing and booming against the cliff bases far below me.

Shortly thereafter, I descended a grassy bluff that led to the north end of Searose Beach, where I decided to have breakfast in a little cobble-filled cove. When I arrived, all the rounded rocks on the upper beach here were very slippery with dew, as they were still in the shadow of the small hill to the southeast. But as my oatmeal cooked, the sun rose over the hill and began to warm both me and the rocks.

Along this part of the coast, cobbles or beach rocks are relatively homogeneous in color due to the area's geology. The vast majority of them are a slate-gray color when dry—these are derived from the central coast's volcanic basalt cliffs and headlands. Here and there, though, there are cobbles that are a light brown color, and others that are almost black, with many white linear crystals embedded in them. The brown ones are from much softer sedimentary rock, and the blackish ones are from a volcanic rock other than the common gray basalt.

After the sun's arrival in the cove, the entire cobbled area between me and the sun shimmered shiny and black for a few minutes, then slowly changed as the rocks began to heat up in the sunshine and evaporate the dew. At first, there were just a few pockets of dull gray rocks amid the sea of still-shiny black ones. After a little while, most of the cobbles had turned gray—at least on their tops and their south-facing sides—but their shady north sides remained wet and dark.

Meanwhile, I ate my first course (the oatmeal) and began to prepare the second: a scrambled egg provided for me by Oleander, one of three hens who live with me back in the Willamette Valley on the other side of the Coast Range. The appearance of the cobbles continued to change, with more and more of them a dull gray and fewer and fewer of them a shiny black.

By the time I moved on to my third course—a sliced quarter-bagel toasted in butter in the frying pan, then topped with blackberry jam—almost all of the cobbles had lost their mantle of dew. And now, as I enjoy my last course here in the glorious sunshine—a pot of Double Bergamot Earl Grey tea—the only shiny, dark cobbles that remain are a few dozen along a little rivulet a hundred feet away.

Watching rocks dry is of course something anyone can do. It takes no special skill—just time and an uncluttered mind . . . two commodities that for many people these days are often in short supply.

DESCENT FROM LØNAHORGI *

AFTER GRADUATING FROM HIGH SCHOOL, I spent the summer in Norway where I lived for most of the time with a host family in the fjord-side village of Fana, less than an hour south of the west-coast city of Bergen. Because life around the house and in the village was not particularly stimulating, I invented activities to keep my mind and body active. Rain or shine, I was out exploring the surrounding, moss-carpeted spruce forests, or climbing nearby Fanafjell, where I had a magnificent view of the area's fjords and mountains.

But the best part of the summer was when my group of a dozen young Americans, scattered at homesites all around west-central Norway, took a bus trip—each of us taking along a Norwegian "brother" or "sister"—that began in Bergen and ended in Oslo two weeks later. We spent our days hiking together, picking wild berries, and visiting sites of historic and cultural significance. Along the way, we stayed in hostels where we received our evening meal, breakfast, and a packed lunch.

Late in the afternoon of our first day on the road, we arrived at a hostel just north of Voss, a popular ski-resort town about fifty miles inland from Bergen. The next morning, at the suggestion of the hostel owner, a party of about a dozen of us took off early to climb Lønahorgi, the nearby mountain visible from the hostel.

Carrying only our lunches, cameras, and some extra clothing in case of inclement weather, we spent the entire forenoon ascending the relatively

* pronounced *le(r)-nah-HOOR-ghee*

gentle southeast shoulder of the peak. Because Norway was heavily glaciated during the most recent Ice Age, most of its mountains have rounded shoulders and broadly domed summits—no sharp ridgetops or pointed, young volcanoes. Near the top, we encountered a mossy boulder the size of a pick-up truck sitting in the middle of a soggy meadow, in the lee of which we sat down and had our lunches out of the wind. (I'm certain I didn't realize it at the time, but given what I now know about glaciation, the boulder was likely a "glacial erratic" deposited there when the ice-cap covering Lønahorgi melted.)

By the time we had finished our lunches, the peak's summit was clouded over and a light mist had begun to fall. Most of the group decided to go back the way we had come up, following the gentle slope in a broad arc back to the valley bottom. But I agreed to join three of the other American guys who wanted to take the "shortcut" back: right down Lønahorgi's steep east flank.

It was a lot of fun at first, as we raced downhill, dodging the scattered boulders along our way while keeping our eyes on the hostel far below, which we were certain to reach before the rest of the group. As the descent got steeper, and we each sought what we thought was the easiest way down, I got separated from the others. Now and again, though, I caught a glimpse through the mist of a bright yellow windbreaker or a blue daypack. But soon I was completely alone. That was okay, since I was accustomed by then to exploring wild areas by myself—as I'd done the previous weeks back in Fana.

My feeling of exhilaration at the beginning of the descent slowly gave way to anxiety, however, as I reached a part of the mountain that was very steep, indeed, and composed mostly of solid rock faces. More than once, I reached an impasse and had to go back uphill a little bit to try another way.

Finally, I got to a spot where I was just plain stuck. I'd jumped down to a little ledge, only to discover that I couldn't go down any farther—it was just too steep. But neither could I get back up the way I'd come. I thought of yelling for help, but the whole mountainside was by then enveloped in a cloud and no one—even if my shouts could be heard—would be able to see where I was.

I had no choice but to jump down to the next ledge—a good ten feet or more below. To improve my balance during the jump, I first tossed my daypack down—with my camera in it—and watched it bounce, then roll off the little ledge and some sixty feet down the rocky slope below, before it finally stopped. I hoped to be luckier than that. First, I sat down so my dangling feet would be a *little* closer to their destination, perhaps providing me with an advantage I wouldn't otherwise have. All I could think of was landing on my feet, and then the rest of my body collapsing onto my shoe tops as all my bones broke from the impact.

I couldn't put it off any longer. I gently launched myself downward, depending on little but Providence to carry me through. I landed on my feet with a dull thud—but I did *not* bounce and roll off the ledge as my pack had. I couldn't believe it. What a relief!

Farther downslope, I retrieved my daypack, then had to face a nearly impenetrable barrier of shrubby birches and junipers that covered the rockfall at the base of the cliff. While fighting my way through that thicket—and not truly knowing in which direction I was going—I also had to be extremely careful not to put my foot down between two boulders and risk breaking a leg.

I eventually reached an open, grassy area where I rejoined the other guys— all of whom had made it down safely, with only one banged-up elbow among the three of them. The rest of our descent was still really steep, but since the slope was grass-covered, I was able to just sit down sometimes and slide on my rear end.

We walked back into the hostel at 6:15 p.m.—long after the rest of the hikers who had taken the "long way," and just in time for supper. Later that evening, I wrote in my journal of the "brush with death" that I'd had earlier. Despite that, or perhaps because of it, I felt that day the most *alive* I had ever felt so far during my eighteen years on the planet. It was a mighty good feeling that I would end up having many, many more times in the coming years.

(This essay, written in 2009, was based in large part on my journal entry from 25 July 1970)

DISCOVERING DANDELIONS

EVERY YEAR IN MID-APRIL, I take my Trees Across Oregon students to Skinner Butte Park in downtown Eugene for our first off-campus field trip of the term. Spring is usually going strong by then, with the cottonwoods leafing out along the river at the base of the butte, and wildflowers such as trillium and false Solomon's seal in full bloom in the coniferous woodland on the butte's northern slope.

It's a fifteen-minute bicycle ride from campus to our meeting spot, and because many students have a class just before mine, they end up arriving a bit late. I always wait for them, and I take advantage of the extra minutes to talk with students who were first to arrive, and answer questions that have come up since the previous class.

Last year, as I wandered among the thirty or forty students who were lounging on the sun-drenched lawn, two of them called me over to show me something. They were sitting cross-legged on the grass and lined up in front of them were eight or ten just-picked dandelion heads. The young man pointed to the dandelions and said to me, "Look what we just discovered!" His female companion then went on to explain that, as they were sitting there surrounded by blooming dandelions and English lawn daisies, they noticed that the yellow-headed dandelions in full bloom and the fluffy seed-heads were actually the same plant, just at different stages of development. And they had arranged in a row all the different stages between flower and seed-head that they had found growing around them.

The two students were just beaming over their discovery. I initially thought to myself that they must be teasing me, but I quickly realized that they were quite serious. I didn't know what to say. I couldn't comprehend that two eighteen-year-olds were learning so late in life what I had learned probably as a toddler. But I smiled at them and said something like, "You're very observant—I'm glad to see that!"

Since then, I've thought a lot about what happened and how we all learn about our surroundings in different ways, at different times, and to differing degrees. As a naturalist in my fifties, I continue to learn things about my surroundings almost daily. My eyes and other senses are wide open to what is going on in my environment—that's just who I am. Occasionally, someone else points out something new to me. But most of the time, I make discoveries all on my own—and those are, for me, the most gratifying.

While this essay was still in draft form, I happened to take some of my current Trees Across Oregon students on a walk north of campus, during which one of the young men came up to me and said: "Whitey, will you settle something for us?" (He was holding a dandelion flower in one hand and a dandelion seed-head in the other.) He said that he thought they were two different plants, but a friend of his in the same group claimed they were just two different stages of the same plant.

I couldn't believe my ears. But I answered his question, then asked for a show of hands: "How many of you never knew this before?" To my utter astonishment, twelve of the fourteen students in my group raised their hands! On top of that, I learned later from my teaching assistant, Nate— who had also been leading a group through the same area at the same time—that one of *his* students raised the very same question!

I've discussed this dearth of dandelion knowledge with several colleagues and friends, and no one can make any sense of it. Almost all of the students in my class come from families who took them hiking and camping during their younger years. But I am also aware that, for most of them, my class is the first time that they have been encouraged to truly open their eyes to the world around them and improve their observation skills.

One friend suggests that the students were likely raised in suburbs of chemically-dependent—and thus dandelion-free—lawns, so they never got to know the plant. And their "nature experiences" with their families took them to wild areas or higher elevations in the mountains where dandelions don't grow. She may be right.

Whatever the case, I'm now redoubling my efforts to open my students' eyes to The-World-Around-Us, so that the remainder of their lives will be filled with discoveries about all kinds of things—now that they finally know about dandelions.

THE MOUND-BUILDERS OF FOLEY RIDGE

MANY NATURE ENTHUSIASTS these days depend on professional guides and "birder hotlines" to take them to where the action is. They don't want to sit around waiting for things to happen. Instead, they prefer to call 1-800-BIRDERS or 1-800-HOTBIRD (!) and be told exactly where the rare Eurasian godwit can be seen. Then they hop in their RV, dial in the GPS setting they got online, and head on out.

Some of us, however, prefer an approach said to be pioneered by Canadian naturalist, Ernest Thompson Seton (1860-1946), more than a century ago. Appropriately called "Seton watching," it involves nothing more than sitting down somewhere for an extended period—say, an hour or two—and watching what happens. The Real World, you see, isn't anything like the National Geographic channel—each program of which, by the way, takes countless hours of "Seton watching" (and filming) to produce.

So here I am, once again, spending a Thursday in the woods, doing absolutely nothing. I'm seated on my forest-green wool blanket in an open stand of 150-year-old Douglas-firs at an elevation of about 2,000 feet in the West Cascades. (The blanket was a birthday gift more than twenty years ago from my mother, who said she never knew what to get for someone like me who claims he doesn't "need" anything—if only she knew how much use this blanket has gotten.)

While enjoying my picnic lunch, I glimpsed out of the corner of my eye some movement on the forest floor just fifteen feet away from me. A small, furry snout! Then it disappeared. A few moments later, there it was again, popping out of the ground beneath a small salal plant. This time, I saw its blunt head as well as half of its chunky, brown body. "Some kind of vole," I thought to myself. Interesting!

Minutes passed, and my sandwich disappeared from my lunchbox into my mouth. Then I saw the animal appear again on the other side of the salal. This time, it emerged from underground, scooted a foot or two away, and chomped off a salal leaf. Then, like a movie being shown in reverse, it speedily ran *backwards* to its burrow and disappeared once again. It was a pocket gopher! They're very stout little rodents, much larger than mice, but smaller than ground squirrels. They have tiny external ears, a short tail, and relatively massive-looking jowls. Although I've seen plenty of *evidence* of these gophers over the years I've visited the ridge, I never actually *saw* one of them until today, as they spend most of their lives underground.

The pocket gopher exited its burrow several more times, each time to fetch a single salal leaf, then scamper in reverse back down into its burrow, holding the big, evergreen leaf in its mouth. There was a period of inactivity for a while. Then I saw something reddish-brown being heaved onto the needle-covered forest floor: fresh loam. The gopher was excavating soil from its burrow and pushing the soil with its head and forelegs onto the forest floor. Within about five minutes, more than a quart of gorgeous loam had been piled into a little mound just inches from the burrow entry.

Unlike the soil mounds made by moles—another subterranean mammal (although not a plant-eating rodent like the gopher, but an "insectivore") whose mounds are perfectly hemispherical and are pushed up from vertical tunnels beneath the mounds' centers—the mounds of pocket gophers have a more irregular shape, with a broad, flattened side facing the burrow's entrance, and a much steeper slope on the "dump" side of the mound away from the entrance.

And unlike the *enormous* mounds made by some pre-Columbian civilizations in the Midwest—such as those nearly 100 feet tall at Cahokia Mounds State Historic Site in southern Illinois—the mounds of these pocket gophers are truly diminutive. But considering the number and size of the workers (one tiny mammal per mound), the little piles of soil are quite impressive.

I smiled to myself as the excavation work continued. Once again, my countless hours of "Seton watching" had paid off: I got to witness one of Foley Ridge's mysterious mound-builders in action!

WHAT I WEAR IS WHO I AM

ONE EVENING, ON THE WAY HOME from my weekly day in The Woods, I had about twenty minutes between connecting buses at Eugene Station, so I decided to walk across the street to the Eugene Public Library to glance at that day's newspaper. As usual on my days in The Woods, my attire consisted of hiking boots, beltless Levi 501 jeans, and a heavy-duty "hickory" shirt—worn here in the Northwest mostly by loggers, or others of the so-called working class. Plus, I had a large, red frame-pack on my back and carried a hiking stick. I was clean-shaven, my clothes and my body were odorless—having had a swim in the McKenzie River just before catching the bus back to Eugene—and my pack was tidy.

As I made my way to the newspaper reading room, I became increasingly conscious that my presence was making some library patrons uncomfortable. One young mother glanced up at me as I walked by, and pulled her two children closer to her. A well-dressed elderly man stepped much farther out of my way than he needed to, as we passed in an aisle. Other people, however, seemed to ignore me—or at least treat me as they would anyone else.

After only a few minutes, it was *I* who had become uncomfortable with my own presence there. Because of Eugene's large population of homeless people, some of these men and women spend their days at the library, where it is safe and clean and warm. Many of them carry their belongings in duffel bags or a large backpack. Was I being "branded" a homeless person because of my attire? I didn't know for sure, but I certainly had the impression that, despite my tidiness and my smile, I was putting off some

18

patrons. So I went back outside to await my connecting bus across the street at the bus station.

The following Monday, I was headed to my classroom at the University of Oregon where I teach. I was wearing what I call my "professor costume": shiny dress shoes; black, creased dress pants with a nice belt; and a long-sleeved, ironed, canary-yellow, button-down Oxford shirt. Over my right shoulder, I carried a navy-blue satchel or "carry-on bag," and in my hand was a carousel of slides to accompany the day's lecture.

As I strode through the main hallway in the School of Architecture building, many of the students and faculty members I passed—most of whom I did not know—looked at me and smiled or nodded hello. More than a few of them purposely made room for me to pass in the crowded hallway and acknowledged me, again, with a smile or a nod. I have become accustomed to this almost reverential behavior when I'm on campus, and when I'm "dressed up." But why the huge difference from how I had been treated only a few days before?

When I'm wearing one of my other hats—as a gardener for both commercial and residential properties—some passersby respond to me just like some of the library patrons did. They see me arrive by bicycle with my coiled garden hose and all my other tools, dressed in Levis and work shoes and a work shirt, and wearing a baseball cap. They watch as I put on my work gloves and proceed to pick up litter around the property, hose vomit off the sidewalk, or put my hands in the dirty (!) soil to plant something or to remove a weed.

Some passersby say hello to me, or have a kind word to say about my handiwork. Others, however, seem to go out of their way to ignore me. And one Sunday morning, as I worked at The Collegian—an off-campus, "upscale" dormitory-like residence—a young man actually spit at me from an upper balcony. (He missed me by just a couple of feet, thank goodness.) I couldn't know, of course, whether I was just a convenient target for him to show off to his girlfriend standing next to him, or if his behavior was actually a put-down.

Most of us, including myself, judge each other—to a lesser or greater extent—based on the clothes we wear. It's unfortunate and sometimes unfair. Those of us with "multiple personas"—in my case, hiker (or homeless person) carrying a backpack, professor, and landscape worker—are more likely to be aware of this than people who do the same kind of work all of the time, or who dress the same way from one day to the next.

As a result of these experiences, I plan to make more of an effort not to judge my fellow humans by the clothes they wear. Sure, my head is still likely to turn when I see an attractive, well-groomed man in a nice business suit. But I'll work extra-hard to see past the dirty coveralls of an unshaven construction worker, to find the human being beneath who deserves just as much acknowledgment and respect from me as the cute guy in the tie.

MANAGING THE HUMAN HERD

I**T'S ELK SEASON** here in Oregon's West Cascades, and the back roads of national forest lands are lively with pick-up trucks, the occupants of which hope to spot a bull elk. I have no quarrel with these hunters—except the few who make an unreasonable amount of noise or who leave litter in their wake. In fact, I admire those (the majority) who are hunting to fill their freezers back home with meat for their families.

Oregon's Department of Fish and Wildlife, along with wildlife biologists here on national forest lands, do an excellent job, in my opinion, of managing our state's elk herd. Elk, after all, nearly became extinct by the late 1800s due to uncontrolled hunting by Oregon's early Euro-American settlers. But these days, elk can be found in almost every county—the larger Roosevelt elk west of the Cascade Mountains crest, and the somewhat smaller Rocky Mountain elk east of the crest—and thousands are killed each fall during the annual harvest.

Biologists use a variety of methods to ascertain the size of the state's elk herd, and hunting quotas vary from year to year based on this information. Over the last couple of decades, the herd has been stable or increasing slowly in size. Most of the elk killed are "excess" bulls, since a single bull can impregnate a whole harem of cows. Sure, in the absence of human hunters, the elk would presumably do just fine, too. But this way, human needs or wants—meat and/or "trophy" antlers—are met without apparently affecting the size and overall health of the herd.

Obviously, I'm very comfortable with this approach to managing the population of one of Oregon's more "charismatic megafauna." And, of course, populations of turkeys, salmon, crabs, and many other animals that humans eat—or find useful for other reasons—are managed in a similar fashion. Over the years, we've gotten pretty good at this.

One of the reasons our society allows and even encourages hunting, especially of larger animals such as deer and elk, is to control those animals' populations. In the absence of human predation, a combination of natural predators and limited forage would work together to accomplish this. Biologists talk about the land's "carrying capacity" or how many animals it can support without degrading the ecosystem. In the absence of natural predators—or human hunters—too many deer, for example, can dramatically affect forest development by eating most of the young tree seedlings growing on the forest floor. Forests east of the Great Plains have a variety of ecological problems due to a surplus of deer—and a dearth of natural predators as well as human hunters these days. In that more densely populated portion of the country, the automobile has assumed the role of "major predator," and it is said that there are *still* too many deer. In other words, the land's carrying capacity is being exceeded.

Interestingly, although concerns about *human* populations exceeding the *planet's* carrying capacity have been expressed for many decades, rarely have those discussions included "management" of the human herd's numbers. Sure, we hear talk about making artificial contraception more widely available, but there is no general agreement on what the planet's carrying capacity for humans *is*, nor how we might purposely stabilize or reduce our own numbers, instead of just letting "nature" take its course.

The subject I've brought up here—the idea of reducing the human population, not just by preventing pregnancies but by "culling" of the ever-growing herd—is completely taboo in contemporary culture. But it hasn't always been like this in every society. Until contact with European cultures, Polynesians, for example, were adept at keeping their populations at or below each island's carrying capacity. They *had* to. Although life was relatively easy on these tropical islands—with an abundance of seafood and cultivated foods—the Polynesians recognized that there were limits to what both nature and their agricultural efforts could provide.

In their earliest centuries, as they moved ever eastward from Indonesia, Polynesians managed their populations partly by war and partly by out-migration. When one island got overcrowded, part of that island's population loaded up the great sea-going, double-hulled canoes and headed out across the Pacific in search of new islands to colonize. Eventually, however, all the habitable islands were occupied. When the first explorers and later missionaries landed in Tahiti, they were horrified to learn of the widely used practices of human sacrifice and infanticide. But as abhorrent as those practices are to modern minds, they were necessary for the Tahitians—and other South Pacific island nations—to maintain a population whose needs didn't exceed the available resources.

Some people would aver that contemporary societies—including the U.S.—already practice infanticide due to the relatively widespread availability of abortion to terminate unplanned or unwanted pregnancies. But what about the rest of us—in our ever-increasing numbers—who are already born and who continue our spread across the planet? How might we stabilize or reduce the existing human population to bring it more in line with what the Earth can truly support?

Bring back human sacrifice? Maybe not. But why can't we have a rational discussion about human beings and the planet's carrying capacity, and then decide how to achieve our goals? As mentioned above, we already accept doing this for *other* species. Why should we humans exempt our own species from purposeful population management?

With every year that passes, more wildlife habitat disappears in Oregon—and virtually everywhere else in the world—to make room for more humans and our buildings, our highways, and our agricultural lands. Out of respect for all the other species with which we share this wondrous planet, it's time for us to begin to manage the human herd as if our lives—and the quality of those lives—depended on it. Because they do.

THE IMPORTANCE OF HYPHENS
AND DIAERESES *

MOST OF US KNOW A LITTLE MORE about one or two subjects than the *hoi polloi*, and we enjoy playing the role of "expert"—even if our knowledge of a particular topic is barely beyond that of the average person. You know how it is: once you've become interested in "birding" and can finally distinguish a sparrow from a finch (based on the shape of their bills, of course), your friends will be asking you all kinds of questions about birds. You'll delight in doing your best to answer them, and your friends will delight in being personally acquainted with an expert such as yourself.

Over the course of a ten-week term in my Trees Across Oregon class at the University of Oregon, I present an enormous amount of information about trees to my students, many of whom seem to have an unlimited capacity for tree facts. And I am very aware of how proud they are to play tree expert for their friends and family. But in my class, they learn much more than how to differentiate a pine from a spruce, and how forest practices ("logging") have changed over the last century.

One of the points I stress is the importance of writing trees' common names and their botanical names correctly. This involves teaching the class about the internationally standardized rules of botanical nomenclature, and a little about English—as well as both Latin and Greek.

---

* pronounced *dye-AIR-ih-seez* (singular *dye-AIR-ih-siss*)

During a campus walk with a group of my students, I pointed out a recently installed bronze commemorative plaque at the base of a newly planted scarlet oak tree. The oak's species name, *coccinea*, was misspelled *coccinia*, tsk-tsk. I reiterated that every tree—just like most of us humans—has a *single* name composed of two parts (genus and species, in the case of plants) that is recognized internationally and is spelled only one way. What if the plaque had misspelled the name of the person being memorialized? It would have been returned to the manufacturer and corrected. But because virtually no one notices the oak's misspelled species name, the mistake persists.

After my little rant about the oak, one of the students in my group asked me if I'd noticed the plaque by a young Douglas-fir in the allée west of Deady Hall. When I said that I had not, he literally beamed as he told me that it was "missing the hyphen." Almost everyone in the group gasped in unison. "How on earth could they not know about the hyphen in Douglas-fir's name?" asked my young experts.

I know very well how-on-earth because I've had that same hyphen removed many times over the years from articles I've written, by editors who thought they knew more about trees than I do. As I had explained to my students earlier in the term, trees' common names can be confusing, and to limit the confusion, we need to spell their names correctly. Douglas-fir, for example, is not what we call a "true fir" of the genus *Abies* (e.g., noble fir and grand fir). It is in a completely different genus (*Pseudotsuga*) and its common name is thus hyphenated, just as we hyphenate Port-Orford-cedar (genus *Chamaecyparis*), which is not a "true cedar" (genus *Cedrus*). Those are the rules, and we need to play by them.

Entomologists (who study insects) do the same thing. A house fly's name is written as two separate words because it is a "true fly" of the genus *Musca*. But dragonflies and butterflies are completely unrelated to true flies, so their names—which were perhaps hyphenated at some point in the past—are now written as single words. Some dendrologists and foresters already write Douglasfir as a single word, and that usage may come to prevail over time.

Another orthographic tidbit my students delight in is the use of a *diaeresis*. Few people these days even know what this is, but it is the "two dots" over the second of two consecutive vowels that tells the reader/speaker that *both* vowels must be pronounced. About the only place we see it anymore is in the words Noël and naïve, but it used to be used—and very effectively—for words like coöperate and reënter, so one didn't accidentally read them as, say, *coop*-erate and *reen*-ter. In these words, the diaeresis was replaced by a hyphen (co-operate and re-enter) and eventually even the hyphen was dropped.

The place my students meet the diaeresis is in botanical names ending in the Greek suffix –oïdes, which means "resembling." For example, Norway maple is *Acer platanoïdes*, or "maple (*Acer*) with leaves resembling those of *Platanus* (the plane-tree or sycamore)." The pronunciation of the suffix is thus *oh-ee-dess* instead of *oy-deeze*. Although contemporary botanical and horticultural texts—at least in the United States—no longer use the diaeresis, I explain to my students the reason for it, and I use it myself when writing the plants' names longhand. So I'm always tickled when I correct my students' tree identification quizzes and almost *every* student has carefully written -*oïdes*. They simply love using their newly acquired knowledge and skills, especially if it is something that sets them apart from their peers.

I know there are some people who will think that I am creating of my students a team of Spelling Police—at least when it comes to tree names— who will stop at nothing in order to have words spelled and written correctly. But better that, than the laissez-faire attitude that seems to be rampant in our society, where "spelling is less important than simply communicating your message." Or worse, a dependence on a computer's Spell-Check—which does not have most trees' names anyway, and is sometimes just plain wrong.

In a recent article that my English professor sister, Beth, wrote for a journal, she described the color of a sweater as "fuschia"—or at least her editor or Spell-Check did. But the color got its name from the flowering plant's genus name, *Fuchsia*, named for German botanist Leonard Fuchs (1501-1566) and "properly" pronounced FUKE-see-uh, not FEW-shuh. And so it goes.

Thanks in part to my observant students, the university's Department of Campus Planning—which coördinates the installation of commemorative plaques—has now been put on notice to be certain that tree names on all future plaques are spelled correctly . . . or they risk a flurry of e-mails from my Trees Across Oregon students.

SWIMMING LAPS
(OR LENGTHS!)

AFTER MORE THAN TWO DECADES, I stepped into a pool again on Tuesday, 25 October 2005. My friend, Steve, had been swimming laps there over the summer, and he suggested that I give it a try.

For years, I had insisted that I would never engage in exercise simply for the sake of exercise—which to me was the height of boredom. After all, my life included plenty of physical activity. As a car-free person, I bicycled everywhere I needed to go in town. And along with gardening—both for myself as well as for a handful of ongoing, year-round clients—I was in decent shape. But my upper body strength, in particular, was not nearly what it could be. And although I have always been a slender guy, my mid-section had over the years become softer and even protruded a bit when I wasn't being careful to keep up appearances by holding it in.

I'd swum laps briefly during graduate school at Oregon State University, from 1978-80, but it was in an indoor pool and I didn't do it on a very regular basis. Then, when I began Ph.D. work at the University of Wisconsin in Madison in the fall of 1981, I began swimming again—and more regularly—because I couldn't garden year-round in the Wisconsin climate, and neither could I bicycle all of the time. (I also found out that swimming was a great way to meet guys who were both gay and in good shape, which made it even more attractive!)

I could still recall back in 2005 how *good* swimming used to make me feel—even though many years had passed since my Madison days—but I was nonetheless completely unprepared for what happened that Tuesday morning at Eugene's Amazon Pool, a recently renovated outdoor pool just a few blocks from my house. I swam only about 800 yards that day, but when I got out of the pool, and for a couple of hours afterward, I was simply euphoric. Both my body and my mind reacted so positively to the swimming that I decided I wanted it to become a regular habit.

Since Amazon Pool was about to close for the season, I began to look around for other opportunities. Only one municipal outdoor pool stayed open year-round; unfortunately, it was a five-mile bike ride from home. But in spring 2005, I had begun teaching at the University of Oregon, and I found out that faculty members could get a term pass to the Student Recreation Center—and indoor Leighton Pool—for only $60. It was a deal I couldn't pass up. So on 9 November 2005, clad only in my little blue Speedo, I slipped quietly into Leighton Pool and began a routine that has already lasted for nearly four years.

Thanks to my daily journal—which I've kept since 1973—I have been able to look back and see how my swimming routine has developed since fall 2005. I began by swimming *fifty* lengths of the 25-yard-long pool (I've always counted lengths, not laps) twice a week, on Tuesdays and Fridays, for a weekly total of 2,500 yards. I swim mostly breaststroke, with a fifth of the lengths arms-only, to help build my upper body which gets the least exercise otherwise; and another fifth of the lengths elementary backstroke, to ensure that I exercise both sets of opposing arm and back muscles instead of just one set.

One way I amuse myself while swimming back-and-forth and back-and-forth is by counting how many strokes it takes to do a length when using only my arms. When I first started, it took me about fifteen arm-strokes per length, but by October 2006 I was already down to thirteen, and later lowered it even more, to ten. So my upper-body strength was obviously improving.

Another way that I became aware of the physical changes that were occurring in me was a comment made by my LMT (licensed massage therapist), Lynn, in May 2006. She'd last seen me in early October of 2005 before I'd begun swimming. So the next time I went in for my semi-annual massage, I entered the massage room alone, as usual, undressed, got onto "the table," and pulled the white bed-sheet up over my naked body. When Lynn came in a few minutes later, she pulled back the sheet to start working on me and remarked, "Oh, my goodness!" Lynn remembers individual bodies like I remember individual trees, and she could see that my May

2006 body was not the same one she'd seen six months earlier! I had "meat" or muscle-mass where I'd never had it before, especially around my shoulders and in my back. And I had even acquired, for the first time in my life, little pecs (or pectoral muscles) which I've since come to refer to as my *pec-lets* because, even though they're bigger than they used to be, they're still not very impressive.

By early 2007, I was swimming *sixty* lengths on Tuesdays and Fridays, for a total of 3,000 yards per week. Then, in March 2007, "Yellow Cap" entered my life. I usually saw this gorgeous guy—who wore a yellow swim cap and whose real name turned out to be "Matt"—only on Fridays, so I suspected he swam Mondays, Wednesdays, and Fridays. If I were going to get to know The-Hunk-in-Lane-Three any better, I would have to change my routine. So I began swimming *three* days a week—Mondays, Wednesdays, and Fridays, of course—in order to have more opportunities to both see and talk with Matt. Because I would be swimming more days each week, I decided to cut back to *fifty* lengths per day again—which was still a total of 3,750 yards a week, a significant increase. And in August 2007, I bumped back up to *sixty* lengths a day, three days a week—or 4,500 yards—where I've stayed ever since, as that seems to be "enough" for me.

(By the way, nothing ever "developed" with Matt. We occasionally chatted amicably in the locker room and played the little eye-games that gay men play, and one day I walked with him to his lab, where he was finishing up his Ph.D. in physics. But besides our significant difference in age, Matt's idea of outdoor recreation—to give just one example—involved loud, fast motorcycles, whereas I preferred quiet hikes in the woods. So we ended up parting ways before ever getting involved.)

The past few years, my swimming routine has remained unchanged: 1,500 yards three times a week; outdoors at Amazon Pool from mid-May until Halloween, then indoors at Leighton Pool the rest of the year. It's a routine that benefits me enormously, both physically and mentally, and so much so that, whenever I have to miss a swim day, I never feel quite up to par that day. It's hard for me to believe that I once deplored exercise simply for the sake of exercise!

HEARING FALL ARRIVE

I HAD SPENT THE NIGHT in one of my favorite stands of grand old Douglas-firs and western redcedars that I call The Cathedral, and when I awoke at first light and lay there inside my tent anticipating another fine day alone in the woods, what should I hear? Nothing. Absolutely nothing. Not even the sound of my own breathing—which I'd stopped briefly, to concentrate on trying to hear *some*thing. Anything!

Much of the year, nearby Two Trout Creek boisterously makes its way through the middle of The Cathedral on its way down to the McKenzie River about a mile away. But in late summer, Two Trout is dry in many places, and not more than a trickle where it's still flowing above-ground.

After a little while, even though it was still barely light, I heard a small woodpecker (probably a sapsucker) looking for its breakfast of insects in a dead tree trunk: Tap-tap-tap . . . tap-tap-peck-peck. And then it was still again. A few minutes later, the cheerful song—but not yet full-volume—of a winter wren punctuated the quiet. Eventually, once it was daylight, I heard the raucous call of a Steller's jay in the distance, and the brief chatter of a chickaree—a small squirrel that is common in the forests of Oregon's West Cascades. Then it was quiet again.

Although by then I was fully awake, I had no inclination yet to get out from under my down comforter and get dressed. It was such a treat to lie in bed, just smiling at my good fortune to be able to experience what I call total tranquility.

(Back in Eugene—where I live most of the time—the early mornings in my neighborhood can also be wonderfully quiet, at least for an urban area. Still, there is the sound of the refrigerator downstairs; a neighbor's car door as she leaves for work; the commuter traffic on 30th Avenue just two-and-a-half blocks away. And, occasionally, louder sounds such as a police siren, or the infernal blasts of a train's horn. Such unwanted sounds, as well as the lack of people who make the sounds, are the principal reasons I come to The Woods in the first place.)

Perhaps an hour after I first awoke, I heard a new sound: plink! A conifer needle falling from the forest's upper canopy onto my tent's fly. Less than a minute later: plink-plink. *Two* conifer needles! How odd, though, that I had heard none before then, and now three in rapid succession. Hmm. A few moments later, another plink. Only then did I realize what I was in fact hearing: raindrops! I had to laugh out loud.

Every year there is a single day—in Whitey's World, at any rate—where summer "officially" ends and fall begins. That is the day when the first raindrops falling from Heaven kiss my cheeks once again and summer can be considered over. Most years, there will be plenty of warm and even hot, sunny days before the *real* rain arrives in late October or early November, but the long summer drought has for me ended with those first raindrops and will not return until the following June.

During any given summer, between mid-June and late August, it's possible to have a good little rain once or twice. But, for me, the only rain that can truly herald the arrival of fall is one that comes later than August 15th. By that time, day length is already noticeably shorter, and even when summer does "return" after the brief rain, I know it cannot last for more than a few additional weeks.

I'm delighted every year when fall arrives, but more often than not, I am anticipating it due to a weather forecast, or dark clouds I can see myself on the western horizon. This year, however, its arrival was completely unexpected. I'd gone to bed after yet another sunny, dry summer day, and I presumed the following day, September 5, would be similar. What a pleasure to be surprised, instead, by the first raindrops of fall.

A ROADSIDE DISTRACTION

URING VISITS TO MY COASTAL SANCTUARY south of Cape Perpetua, I prefer to get from one place to another by wandering through the woods, walking along the beach, or clambering over grassy headlands. But occasionally, that just isn't possible, and I have to walk along the shoulder of the Oregon Coast Highway.

Early mornings, I have the highway mostly to myself, and that's my preferred time, of course, to hike along it. By mid-morning, however, traffic has usually picked up enough to make my walk, even for short distances, less than pleasant. Although it's just a two-lane highway, with many curves and hills, much of the traffic proceeds at very high speeds. And during the tourist season, from May through October, many of the vehicles are enormous RVs that buffet the rare pedestrian with gusts of air, clouds of dust, and once in a while a stray piece or two of gravel.

During the quieter times of day, I have plenty of opportunities to enjoy the spectacular coastal scenery, admire and smell roadside wildflowers, and even pick thimbleberries or evergreen huckleberries growing just off the highway. I also notice the litter I have to step over, or which I see half-hidden in the vegetation just beyond the graveled shoulder. Because my visits to the coast serve in part to maintain my mental health—by getting me away from my fellow humans and their sometimes noisy and inconsiderate behavior—I make a concerted effort not to be bothered by the trash I see. I "acknowledge" it, so to speak, and then move on to happier thoughts.

Now and then, however, I notice a piece of trash that for some reason merits my further attention. So it was on Saturday, February 21st, this year, as I headed north from Strawberry Hill to Cummins Creek, following the west side of the highway. Almost exactly at milepost 169—or where MP169 *used* to be, as the marker has been removed or stolen since my last visit—a plastic bottle lying atop the roadside gravel caught my eye. I picked it up and found that it had a most peculiar name. The brand of the beverage was Glaceau . . . sounds French! The word *glace* does in fact mean "ice" in French; and *eau* means "water." But "glaceau" means nothing at all. It's probably just another completely fabricated brand name—like Häagen-Dazs, which strives to be Scandinavian, but is not—designed to entice buyers who are simply attracted to European-sounding names.

The next four words in the name left me laughing out loud right there by the road: Nutrient Enhanced Water Beverage. I knew what every one of those four words meant, but I'd never seen them used in that combination before. A glance at the ingredient list transported me back to my college organic chemistry classes. Wow. I could pronounce the chemicals, but I had no idea why anyone would want to ingest them. The list included "electrolytes"—all I could think of was car battery fluid, for some reason. Yuck! I wonder how the human race could have ever prospered before the invention of these so-called "sports" drinks.

The beverage container also brought to mind the curious "hydration fetish" that afflicts so many people these days. Even at the university pool where I swim laps, many of the other swimmers have bottles of their preferred "water beverages" waiting for them at the edge of the pool. Every few laps, they stop briefly and take another swig. Perhaps I'm not realizing my full potential as a swimmer because I'm not squirting some fluid down my gullet every time I turn around?

Meanwhile, you can be sure that I won't be prowling the beverage aisle at the local grocery in search of Glaceau Nutrient Enhanced Water Beverage. When I'm truly thirsty, all I have to do is turn on the faucet in my kitchen and out flows some of the best water there is. It's from the McKenzie River east of Eugene, in whose pristine waters I bathe on an almost weekly basis between April and October. The water I drink may not have any electrolytes or long-named ingredients in it. But it arrives at my house by pipe and is incredibly inexpensive—$1.18 per 1,000 gallons, or less than an eighth of a cent per gallon. Thankfully, I appear to be flourishing as a result of drinking it regularly!

THE QUEST FOR QUIET CONTINUES
Aural Snapshot No. 11

I T'S ANOTHER LOVELY DAY on the ridge, with only occasional sprinkles and the temperature in the upper 50s. In the distance is the muffled sound of the McKenzie River about a mile away. Here in this stand of twenty-year-old Douglas-firs, it's mostly silent except for the gentle chirping of late-season crickets. Time for another Aural Snapshot, where for one hour I note what different sounds I hear for each minute of the hour.

Very few people these days have or take the opportunity to expose themselves to "natural silence." I don't mean the absence of any sound whatsoever, because one can experience that in the middle of a city inside a soundproofed room such as a recording studio or a movie theatre. Rather, *natural* silence is simply the absence of any *human*-associated sounds, from music and the barking of dogs, to leaf blowers, garbage trucks, and aircraft.

Spending time in the woods alone—or with someone else who is comfortable being quiet—is a wonderful way to experience natural silence, especially if one avoids moving water, the sound of which can hinder appreciation of other, more subtle natural sounds. So here goes!

*   *   *   *   *   *

The hour is now up. What did I hear? In descending order of the number of minutes during which each kind of sound was heard at least once, here is the tally:

18 minutes	aircraft (14 minutes jet, 4 minutes propeller)
15 minutes	frog
15 minutes	chickaree (type of squirrel)
11 minutes	red-breasted nuthatch
6 minutes	winter wren
5 minutes	wind gust in trees
5 minutes	raven
5 minutes	fly
4 minutes	chickadee (type of bird)
4 minutes	junco
2 minutes	pine siskin (type of bird)
2 minutes	evening grosbeak
1 minute	pileated woodpecker
(9 minutes)	(unidentified sounds)

As usual, the calls of birds—from wrens to ravens—dominated the hour. But the sound of the largest winged critter of all (aircraft) dominated almost a third of the hour. And unlike most natural sounds, aircraft noise is *constant* during the minutes it is present. On average, aircraft are audible for nearly thirty of every sixty minutes during a typical weekday because the otherwise mostly pristine Cascade Mountains have the misfortune of lying directly below a major north-south flight path (see map on next page).

Friends who live in rural parts of Oregon and elsewhere in the U.S. tell me that they seldom *hear* aircraft—and that when they *see* aircraft overhead, the planes are "too high to hear." Such claims suggest to me that my friends have become inured to the sound of aircraft; or that natural sounds such as wind and moving water may be obscuring the aircraft noise. I know very well, because the commercial jets I am hearing today are flying at altitudes well above 20,000 feet (about four miles), and possibly as high as 30–35,000 feet (or six to seven miles). And back in Eugene, under certain meteorological conditions, I can sometimes hear the sound of aircraft taking off from Eugene's airport, which is located *ten* miles from my house.

So where would I have to go in Oregon to get away from aircraft noise? According to the map, the Kalmiopsis Wilderness in southwestern Oregon's Siskiyou Mountains would be a good bet—which is corroborated by a friend who has camped there many times and always been grateful for the silence, compared to the Cascades. I know from my own experience that the Coast Range west of Eugene is also relatively quiet. Alas, neither of these spots is easy to get to with public transportation, so I must settle for the "sometimes quiet" West Cascades, served four times daily by a bus from Eugene.

Many people might think that the sparsely populated desert of southeastern Oregon would be the quietest place in the state. But a quick glance at the flight path map shows otherwise. So these days, peace-and-quiet (or natural silence) is a relative term. And unless and until we collectively decrease our "need" for air travel—business, vacations, a death in the family, etc.—and stop demanding "overnight mail" and the like, it's going to be ever harder to find.

*　　　*　　　*　　　*　　　*　　　*

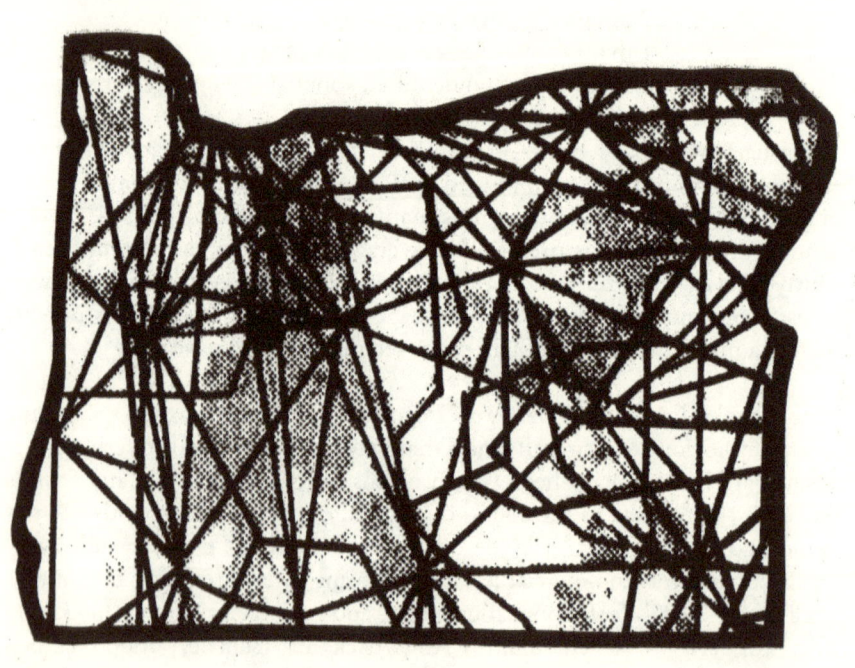

Flight paths over Oregon designated by the Federal Aviation Administration. Adapted from Appendix D in Gordon Hempton's One Square Inch of Silence *(© 2009). Sharp-angled lines may indicate flight paths for aircraft engaged in military training exercises. The large black dot indicates the location for most of my aural snapshots, approximately sixty miles east of Eugene.*

(This aural snapshot was recorded on 5 November 2009.)

WHERE HORNETS COME TO DRINK

IT'S A SIMPLY SWELTERING DAY here in the West Cascades. Even in the deep shade beneath 200-foot-tall conifers—and at the base of a north-facing slope—the temperature mid-afternoon is 90 degrees. That means that it's perhaps 100 degrees out in clearings and on south-facing slopes, places I stay away from on days like this.

After finishing my lunch at the base of an old Douglas-fir, I decided I needed to find a cooler spot to spend the rest of the afternoon. One option was to return to the McKenzie River valley—where I got off the bus several hours ago—and string up my hammock next to the cold, fast-flowing river where air temperatures are always ten or twenty degrees cooler. But that meant hiking down off the ridge in the heat of the day, and exposing myself to the dreaded end-of-the-day highway noise far sooner than I wanted to. Plus, the river in the summertime attracts numerous people in brightly colored rafts and kayaks and other watercraft, the sight and sound of which I would rather not experience on my weekly peace-and-quiet day.

Thankfully, I had another option. Less than fifty feet away from my lunch spot was tiny Two Trout Creek, a perennial stream—i.e., it flows year-round, unlike many small "seasonal" creeks in the West Cascades that flow only in winter and spring—which I've come to know well over a quarter century of visits to this area. The temperature of the creek, even in mid-summer, seldom exceeds fifty degrees. And although it's now very small and intermittent, running underground for short stretches before resurfacing, its cold water, like that of the much larger McKenzie, creates a special microclimate that is quite pleasant on a hot summer day.

I packed up my things, slid my feet into my hiking boots, and came down here to a little creekside gravel bar just big enough for me and my backpack. After sitting still for a few minutes, I began to feel the difference. Although there is a strong *uphill* wind of hot, dry air in the upper forest canopy, here by the little creek, there is a gentle *downhill* breeze of cool, moist air. I took out my field thermometer and discovered, first, that the water temperature is an unusually warm 54 degrees. Just six inches above the water, where my hips are, the air temperature is 72°. At shoulder level, it's 82°. And just above my head, it's 86°. Sitting up, then, I justifiably feel a little "hot-headed" because of the temperature differential, but it's very tolerable.

Unlike forests east of the Great Plains at this season, there are virtually no biting insects here. The few mosquitoes and no-see-'ems of early summer are now gone here at an elevation of 1,800 feet, though they're exceedingly abundant higher up in the Cascades—where you'll never find *me* in mid-summer—due to countless snowmelt ponds and lakes that provide nurseries for the insects' larvae until late August or early September.

Although many people refer to these forests as "rain forests," they really aren't. A good deal of precipitation falls between November and March most years, but the forests become very dry by mid-summer, and creeks are few and far between at that season. The coastal Fog Belt, on the other hand—home of Oregon's only *true* rain forests—is bathed in summer almost daily by fog. Creeks there are more numerous, and soil moisture levels can remain relatively high throughout the summer "drought."

So here in the West Cascades, even tiny streams like this one become lifelines for a host of wild creatures, from insects and birds, to deer and bear. While sitting here for over an hour, I've watched one insect in particular come on a regular basis to nature's drinking fountain. It's about one inch long, mostly black, with a white head, and white, too, on the tip of its abdomen. The insect is called a bald-faced hornet.

Today is the first day this year that I've seen them, and they're right on schedule, as every year they appear in these forests in mid-summer, then disappear again in early fall. Presumably, an impregnated queen overwinters, perhaps in a rotten log, then re-emerges in spring to find a nest site and begin laying eggs that will hatch into "worker" hornets. I had a memorable encounter with these hornets over a decade ago, when I inadvertently disturbed a nest and suffered a half-dozen very painful stings. In fact, for years following that incident, I seldom visited these woods in summer anymore because of an unfounded fear of bald-faced hornets. Eventually, however, I got over it when I realized that most of the hornets I encounter are solitary, foraging females who are simply too busy with their work to worry about me, and even though it did happen once, the chance of disturbing one of their "paper"-covered, above-ground nests again is truly remote.

While I've spent the past couple of hours refreshing myself in the cool creekside air—and occasionally splashing some of the water on my arms—the hornets have been coming and going, and refreshing and rehydrating themselves with tiny sips from the same creek. What a treat it's been for me on this hot summer day to peacefully share this precious resource with my former "enemies," the bald-faced hornets.

A FEW FACTS ABOUT WESTERN OREGON'S
ILL-DESERVED RAINY REPUTATION

MANY PEOPLE IN WESTERN OREGON seem to have the impression that wintertime—the wettest four months of the year, from early November through late February—is one endless deluge. They complain to one another about the "constant gray skies" and the moss and lichens that grow on everything. Interestingly, despite the seasonal gloom that they say pervades this part of the state, the same people often delight in bragging to visitors and to each other about how many consecutive rainy days there were last winter and the fact that they survived with their sanity intact.

Unfortunately, these rainy-day tales are simply not true. First of all, the Willamette Valley—where most Oregonians live—is in the so-called rain shadow of the Coast Range to the west. Were it not for these mountains, valley cities like Eugene, Salem, and Portland would likely receive about the same rainfall as coastal communities: some seventy-five inches per year. But the annual precipitation for most valley communities is less than forty inches.

Sure, there are rainy periods every winter, some lasting a few days or occasionally a week or more. But there are also extended periods each winter when it does NOT rain, lasting some years for up to several weeks. Why do people seem to forget these dry times?

Many people know that I go to The Woods on Thursdays, and quite a few of them like to accompany me every week—at least vicariously. Whenever it's a rainy Thursday in Eugene, they "feel sorry" for me up in the West

Cascades, having to "slog" through the woods on a wet day, and they make a point of telling me so either before I leave ("The forecast says . . . ") or after my return ("It must have been just *awful* up there on Thursday . . . ").

I have never let the occasional rainy day stop me from enjoying The Woods. I just carry an umbrella, wear rubber boots, and when it comes time to sit down and enjoy my lunch or take a nap, I put up my little brown tarp, snuggle under my wool blanket, and smile the day away. But there really are relatively few rainy Thursdays in a given winter.

I have kept a daily journal for nearly thirty-seven years now—and a special "upriver" journal since the early 1990s—in which I note each day's weather with a little symbol denoting sunniness, cloudiness, and relative amount of rain or snow. To get some idea of the actual frequency of wet days, I checked back through my upriver journals.

I chose the years 2000-2009 and first tabulated the total number of Thursdays that I spent upriver during our four-month winters. I then determined the number of "wet" days, whether there was just a spit of rain or a downpour, or a flurry of snow or a blizzard. And here is what I found: Over those forty winter months—four months each year, over ten years—I spent 136 Thursdays in The Woods, and during only 37 of them (barely more than a quarter) did *any* precipitation fall. Conversely, 99 of the 136 days were completely dry.

Were I to do the same tabulations for *all* 1200 winter days—four 30-day months each year, over ten years—for that same period, I am confident that the result would be very similar. In other words, the weather for an entire winter of *Thursdays* is representative of the weather for that same winter if I were to include *all* of the days.

It is true that during the past decade, the Pacific Northwest has been experiencing one of its periodic dry cycles. During this time (2000-2009), not a single winter in Eugene has exceeded even the *average* winter precipitation calculated for the previous three decades (1971-2000). But the fact remains that even during a wetter part of the climate cycle, there are plenty of dry days scattered among the wet ones each winter.

I think there are several reasons for the constant commentary among the locals about western Oregon's raininess. First, as in other parts of the country and the world, the weather in general provides a safe and easy topic for conversation—as opposed to, say, politics, sex, or the economy. Second, weather that strays from the norm—especially if it creates an inconvenience for people—is far more likely to be remembered than those "nice" days when the sun shines and it's neither too hot nor too cold (nor too wet) to be comfortable outside. And third, let's face it, people are prone to exaggeration, the level of which tends to increase with the amount of time that has elapsed since the event(s) occurred.

Yes, western Oregon has a winter-wet, summer-dry (or "Mediterranean") climate—just like Marseille and Sacramento—and the majority of its annual precipitation falls in the form of rain during a period of just a few months. But each and every winter, *many* of the days are rainless; and in any particular winter, there are *always* extended rain-free periods, some of them lasting for up to several *weeks*.

So much for western Oregon's "wintertime curse." Now that the truth is out, I'm eagerly looking forward to some stimulating conversation and commentary about politics, sex, and the economy!

CHRISTMAS BREAKFAST COMPANIONS

I AM BLESSED TO LIVE IN A COMMUNITY that has both a river running through it and a mountain overlooking it. Actually, because this is The West and the mountain is a solitary one and not part of a range, we call it a butte: Spencer Butte. Instead of having a revolving restaurant or a communications tower at its summit or a subdivision of posh homes on its upper slopes—as some mountains near urban areas have —Spencer Butte is part of Eugene's superb network of parks and open spaces and is relatively pristine.

Most of Eugene lies at an elevation of 400-500 feet above sea level, on the broad floodplain of the Willamette River, and Spencer Butte's summit is just over 2,000 feet. In winter, when the valley is sometimes filled with a dense, cold fog that can persist for days on end, the top few hundred feet of Spencer Butte are *always* above the fog. And that's good to know.

Winter fog affects people here in a variety of ways: 1) the air is cold (typically in the 30s or low 40s) and damp, so it is uncomfortable to be outside for long; 2) visibility is limited, which can create a claustrophobic feeling; 3) because air movement is just about nil, pollutants from automobiles, wood stoves, and industrial sources build up, affecting air quality and making breathing difficult for some people; and 4) because some of us know that the sun is shining only a thousand or so feet above us—while we're stuck down in the fog—a persecution complex may develop because it just doesn't seem "fair"!

Today is the third consecutive day of fog. The first day, I did my best to ignore it, and grumbled very little. Yesterday, the second day, I went by bus to the McKenzie Bridge area in the West Cascades, 60 miles east of Eugene, which, like the summit of Spencer Butte, is always out of the fog. And this morning, when I awoke and looked outside to see dense fog once again, I decided to head up the butte for breakfast.

After taking care of chores at home—making my bed, feeding the chickens—I packed my things, hopped on my bike, and pedaled the two miles to the Martin Street trailhead at the end of West Amazon Drive. From there, it was a three-mile hike and a 1,500-foot elevation gain to the summit, through a dense forest of Douglas-firs. Less than a quarter mile before the top, however, I reached tree-line and stepped out of the foggy forest into the sunshine!

After another hundred yards of clambering across exposed bedrock, I came to my favorite spot on the butte's steep upper south slope, where there is a rock ledge with a perfect backrest that is out of the north wind and away from other people—most of whom congregate at the very top in a sometimes noisy mix of barking dogs, yelling kids, and loud-talking adults. Here, I set up my little Swedish Optimus stove and got my breakfast underway: hot oatmeal (with dried plums, dried apricots, raisins, and pecans), an egg fried in butter, and Earl Grey tea.

While the oats cooked, I enjoyed the absolute quiet. I am grateful that less than an hour and a half from my front door—I left home at 8:50 and arrived here by 10:15—and within the city limits, I can find the peace-and-quiet that is so essential to my mental health.

As I sat here, I recognized familiar voices nearby and, sure enough, in the treetops just below me was a flock of red crossbills. I often hear these birds at my refuge in the West Cascades where they are year-round residents, but I seldom see them because they forage for conifer seeds high in the forest canopy above me. But here, I happen to be higher than the tops of the trees growing down-slope from me, so I have a grand view of the crossbills.

Interestingly, whenever I encounter crossbills, they are in small flocks of from six to twelve birds—seldom fewer and rarely more—and they are chattering incessantly with each other. As the bird's name suggests, the two tips of its beak (or bill) actually criss-cross—the better, apparently, to extract those reluctant conifer seeds from the cones that hold them.

After watching a flock feeding in a nearby fir for a few minutes, they suddenly took flight, chattering even more excitedly, and as they flew by quite closely, I got a splendid glimpse of the males' brilliant red plumage in the morning sunshine. What wonderful companions—sunshine and crossbills—to have had with my Christmas breakfast!

AROMA-THERAPY

WE HUMANS ARE BLESSED with five wonderful senses—sight, hearing, smell, taste, and touch—all of which can produce very pleasant sensations when stimulated in a suitable fashion. Unfortunately, as we have become increasingly "civilized" in relatively recent times, our senses have suffered.

The greatest loss appears to be our ability to detect subtleties. Many observers find that I have unusually keen senses. I attribute this super-sensitiveness to two personal traits. First, I tend to eschew things that can overwhelm the senses: brightly colored objects and fast-moving images; loud sounds; artificial fragrances; and strongly flavored drinks and foods. And second, I spend an enormous amount of time outdoors, in natural settings—and often alone—where I am able to better exercise my senses and hone them to a fine edge.

My sense of smell rewards me on a regular basis, and I've learned through the years how certain scents can positively affect my outlook. One of the most striking scents often occurs following a prolonged foggy period in the Willamette Valley, when fresh, comparatively warm air arrives from the west to displace the cold, stale air that has gripped the area for days. The air smells sweetly of freshly crushed conifer needles, and its warmth and lower humidity are invigorating after the foggy spell. In a given winter, I might encounter this particular fragrance just once or twice—but it always makes me breathe more deeply and purposefully, and whatever attitude I had before its arrival improves considerably.

On the days that I spend in the woods in the West Cascades, I often find myself seeking out a certain plant to sniff because I know that I will respond favorably to its scent. Soon after stepping off the bus at the McKenzie River Ranger Station of the Willamette National Forest, I often head for a nearby grand fir. I pick half a dozen needles, twist them in my fingers, and inhale the citrus-like fragrance. Many people to whom I've introduced this plant refer to the scent as "Christmas-y" and it kindles for them fond memories, just as it does for me.

Other common forest plants I am regularly drawn to for their "aroma-therapeutic" qualities include yerba buena, wild ginger, cottonwood, thimbleberry, and red-flowering currant. Most people associate fragrance with the *flowers* of different plants, and of course some plants have very aromatic flowers. But the fragrance of the plants I find aroma-therapeutic is produced without exception by these plants' *foliage*.

Yerba buena (*Satureja douglasii*) is an evergreen member of the mint family that grows as a sparse groundcover in open (i.e., somewhat sunny) Douglas-fir woodlands. Its small leaves, when bruised or crushed, emit a delicious minty smell. The common name means "good plant" in Spanish, which is certainly apt, in my opinion.

Wild ginger (*Asarum caudatum*) is a common wildflower in the West Cascades with evergreen, heart-shaped leaves. Although unrelated to culinary ginger, its leaves and rhizomes (underground stems) produce the same gingery smell when crushed. Nice!

The cottonwood (*Populus trichocarpa*) is common along watercourses throughout much of Oregon—both east and west of the Cascade Mountains. As the trees break bud and leaf out in spring, the air on warm days takes on a deliciously balmy scent. In fact, early pioneers called the tree "balm of Gilead," a biblical reference to an unrelated tree whose fragrance was considered "restorative." As much as I look forward to and appreciate cottonwood fragrance every spring, my favorite trick is to pick a still-closed cottonwood bud on a cold, wintry day, then warm it up by rolling it between my warm fingers until it begins to exude its "springtime" fragrance. That always makes me smile!

Thimbleberry (*Rubus parviflorus*) is a thornless relative of blackberries and raspberries with fuzzy, maple-like leaves that are soft and very sensuous. In addition to this tactile attribute is the delicate scent of just-emerging thimbleberry foliage on a sunny, warm spring day. I am greatly enamored of this subtle, lemony scent. One fine spring day, perhaps eight years ago, I was bent over the small thimbleberry patch in my front yard, inhaling its delicious fragrance, when I sensed that I was being watched. I looked up to see my elderly neighbor, Leah, looking at me in a suspicious fashion. I laughed and then explained what I was doing, and invited her to try it herself. She couldn't smell anything—many older people have a diminished sense of smell—and for the rest of her days, I think that she believed me to be just a little crazy.

Red-flowering currant (*Ribes sanguineum*) grows wild throughout western Oregon, especially on sunny and recently disturbed (logged or burned) sites. It is also a popular cultivated plant. As lovely as its flowers are, it is the scent of its newly-emerged foliage in early spring that is really incredible. For that reason, I planted one adjacent to the public sidewalk in front of my house, and I marvel at how many passersby look and look for what *flower* is making that sweetly spicy aroma, when in fact it's the currant bush's *leaves* right in front of them that are so fragrant!

Lastly, there is a small native "animal" whose scent is simply extraördinary. It is a species of millipede about two inches long that is glossy black—or sometimes brown—with a row of bright orange dots down each side of its segmented body. These millipedes are very common in native forests and can sometimes be found in urban settings as well. When picked up and held briefly in the palm of one's hand, they curl up into a spiral and emit an aroma that smells exactly like almond extract. For that reason, I call them "marzipan millipedes" for the almond paste used in many European confections. Long after the millipede has been released, the sweet scent remains on one's hands. What a treat!

So get outside and give your underused sense of smell some exercise. By training yourself to be a better sniffer—and seeking out aromatic foliage and even critters, as well as flowers—you'll open up a whole new world for your enjoyment.

THE SOUND OF BUTTERFLY WINGS
Aural Snapshot No. 12

IT'S A SPLENDID EARLY SPRING AFTERNOON here at an elevation of 2,000 feet in the West Cascades—a couple of miles east-southeast of McKenzie Bridge—and I'm sitting in one of my favorite "day-nests" here at what I call Sixteen Madrones. The sun is shining in a cloudless sky, the temperature is in the upper 60s, and California tortoise-shell butterflies are simply everywhere.

These butterflies are unusually abundant some years—and the cause of their occasional population explosions is unknown. The upper side of their wings is orange-brown with large black spots and dark wing borders; the underside is a dark, mottled brown. And, unlike some butterflies, they are very, very friendly.

Because butterflies prefer sunny landscapes, I didn't see my first tortoise-shells today until I came out of a stand of old conifers, into this open, sunny stand of twenty-year-old trees. It was late forenoon, and the day was still warming up after last night's hard freeze. The butterflies, too, were just warming up, and there were relatively few to be seen.

But by early afternoon, in a quick glance around me, I could count a couple of dozen. Every once in a while, one or two of them would flutter right by my face, or land on my hat or my pant leg. It's so quiet here that I can easily hear their gentle wingbeats, even when they're a yard or two away from me.

What a perfect day for another "aural snapshot," when, for each of sixty consecutive minutes, I note what sounds, if any, I hear—whether each sound occurs only once during that minute, or is repetitive or constant. During the sixty minutes I recorded the sounds below—from 1:50 p.m. to 2:50 p.m.—there was also the constant sound of fallen madrone leaves crackling gently in the warm, dry air, as well as a slight breeze that occasionally ruffled the foliage of both the madrones and nearby Douglas-firs.

Over the course of the hour, I heard only sixteen different sounds—besides the crackling leaves and occasional breeze. One of the sounds occurred during almost every minute of the hour—and one of them occurred only once! Here's the breakdown:

fly	49 minutes
butterfly	40 minutes
woodpecker tapping	31 minutes
hoverfly (a bee-like fly)	24 minutes
Steller's jay	16 minutes
bumblebee	13 minutes
chickadee	13 minutes
raven	9 minutes
gnat	7 minutes
red-breasted nuthatch	7 minutes
golden-crowned kinglet	7 minutes
propeller-driven plane	6 minutes
commercial jet	5 minutes
chickaree (a small squirrel)	3 minutes
northern flicker	2 minutes
my tummy gurgling!	1 minute

Except for the flies and hoverflies, which are a constant presence in clearings on warm, sunny days, it was a blissfully quiet hour. Perhaps most notable of all was the relative absence of aircraft noise—which typically disturbs the tranquility here for nearly thirty out of every sixty minutes—with the sound of their engines today being audible only eleven of the sixty minutes.

But the greatest pleasure of all was the sweet and soft sound of butterfly wings, as the affable tortoise-shells fluttered all around me. Perhaps they were just as delighted to discover an unusually quiet and gentle human being, as I was to get to spend my afternoon with them.

THE TATTOO

I HAD AGREED TO GIVE PETER HIS EXAM early because his parents had inadvertently booked his flight back to the Midwest the day *before* our class final was scheduled. And I had asked him to come to my home, which is close to campus, to take the exam. Peter had already visited my place once—during a neighborhood tree tour that I had led during the seventh week of the ten-week term—and he assured me that he wouldn't have any trouble finding it again. But I e-mailed him my address the day before, just in case.

In anticipation of his 9 o'clock arrival, I cleared the dining room table of breakfast dishes and placed a small glass bowl of floating lawn daisies next to his exam. By 9:15, he still hadn't shown up. Finally, around 9:30, I was beginning to get a little anxious. I had turned off my telephone's ringer—as I always do when I'm expecting a visitor—but I went upstairs to my office to see if, by chance, Peter had called me.

Indeed, there were two messages from him, the second one clearly more frantic than the first. He wasn't able to find my house and had neglected to bring along with him my address. I immediately called him back on his mobile phone and, by chance, as we were talking, I looked outside and saw him pedaling by—one hand on his handlebars and the other holding the phone to his ear. Moments later, he stepped inside my house, literally shaking from having been both late and lost, and his T-shirt was soaked with perspiration.

I couldn't bear to make him sit down to take an exam in such a condition. So we talked a bit and I asked him if he'd had any breakfast. No, he hadn't. I offered to make him some, and he happily accepted. Over buttered toast with honey, and a glass of milk, we talked about his plans for the summer, and he commented on the yellow-centered daisies floating in the bowl: "They look like little sunshines smiling up at us!"

After a few minutes, Peter had settled down enough to take the exam. I went upstairs to work at my desk, so I wouldn't distract him in any way—yet I was nearby, should he have any questions.

Peter was not one of my better students, but like so many of the poorer students, he still loved my class, attended regularly, and said that he had learned a lot. Less than a half-hour after sitting down to the final, he called upstairs to say he was finished. I cursorily looked over his exam. Many spaces were blank; he hadn't even made educated guesses at the answers. I felt sorry for Peter, but his usual cheerfulness didn't appear to be at all dampened by his poor performance on the exam.

We conversed for a few more minutes, and then I took him outside to see my garden and my hens in the backyard. Just before leaving, he said he wanted to show me something. When I smiled and nodded in assent, he reached down and pulled up his pant-leg to reveal a ten-inch-long tattoo of a conifer on his right calf. He looked back up at me and said proudly, "It's a Douglas-fir, Oregon's state tree. I got it to remind me of you and the best class I ever had."

Peter, it turns out, would never return to Oregon from the Midwest. I found out later from a friend of his—who had been in the same class—that he had "flunked out of school." I was saddened, yet not surprised. But then I smiled to think that his Douglas-fir tattoo—the only one I have ever seen—would likely remain with him for the rest of his life. And whenever someone would ask him about it, he would think once again of the year he spent in Oregon, and of the best class that he had ever taken.

BUDDIES, BULLETS, AND BEER

I 'VE COME TO THE WOODS here in the West Cascades for a few days of peace and quiet. It's been too long since I last recharged my batteries by staying outside for more than a day, so this is a welcome treat. To ensure some degree of solitude, I've hiked overland about two miles, to a broad ridge-top where I've set up my tent in an open, grassy area at the end of an abandoned logging road that is gated nearly a mile from here and is thus inaccessible to vehicles.

Around dusk on my first day here, I heard shooting. At first, it was the rapid firing of a small gun—perhaps a pistol. Soon, however, I was startled by the boom-boom-boom of a much larger weapon. The noise seemed to be coming from an old hunting camp off a main gravel road about a half-mile away. I've seen evidence there before of this type of activity, and always counted my blessings that I'd not been around when the people inclined toward such behavior were there.

The series of gunshots were interspersed with periods of quiet. But just when I thought the shooting had stopped for the night, it would recommence. Target shooting is of course legal on public lands, but I wondered how in heaven's name they could still be shooting after nightfall.

Finally, around 10 p.m., I blew out my candle lantern and slid into my sleeping sheet, then pulled my down comforter over me. Good night. Sometime after I'd reached a point of very deep sleep, ka-POW, ka-POW, ka-POW!! They were at it again. There was nothing I could do except turn over and try to go back to sleep.

This morning, though, I went back down to the highway to the ranger station—leaving my camp on the ridge for a couple of hours—to talk with a ranger about what had happened. He reminded me that there was really nothing that could be done, if the people were not shooting at trees or wildlife, and not making a mess of the site. He counseled me just to move my camp, which I agreed would be the best solution.

On my way back up the hill, through the woods, I thought I heard a vehicle descending the little forest road nearby. Hmm. Perhaps the noisy people were leaving. So I decided to hike over to the area where I believed the noise originated. As I approached the site, I saw fresh tire tracks in the mud, as if a vehicle had in fact just left.

Upon closer inspection, I found a just-drowned campfire, some cardboard targets, *hundreds* of spent shells, two burned-out cans of beans, and a dozen or so beer cans—Busch and Budweiser—perforated by bullets. Behind a large tree nearby was a pile of human excrement, next to which were half a dozen used paper napkins with teddy bears on them.

Since guys never, in my experience, engage in this sort of "recreation" alone, I had to assume that there were at least two of them. They were very likely good buddies who'd stopped at the general store back down the highway for bullets, beer, and a couple of cans of baked beans, then drove to the nearest public land they could find, to spend a rip-roaring evening together, sleep it off in the back of the truck, and then head back home the next morning. I suppose it could be seen as just one more example of harmless social behavior that helps people bond.

But these guys ruined *my* evening and *my* night out here—and my early morning, when a few more shots rang out around 7 a.m. And they made a mess of a beautiful piece of public land that belongs to them, yes, but that also belongs to me and you. ("This land is your land, this land is my land, from the redwood forests to the Rio Grande. . . . ") Back in Eugene, I'm exhorted by bumper stickers and weekend workshops to "embrace diversity." And I try. I really do! But somewhere, a line must be drawn. The people who last night shared with me this forested ridge-top crossed that line.

THE MIDDLE OF THE ROAD

ALTHOUGH I PREFER TO GO CROSS-COUNTRY or just follow animal trails when I'm in the woods, I sometimes walk along forest roads. Most of these are gravel, and those that are used very little, or gated to keep vehicles out, often have just two parallel tracks with low-growing vegetation between the tracks. They're very pleasant roads to walk along because of their "intimacy." Often, the roadside vegetation has begun to reclaim the roadways and, with the green median, they really look like twin hiking trails instead of roads.

For the most part, I walk on one or the other of the little gravel "trails" instead of in the median, to avoid needlessly crushing any vegetation beneath my feet. Sometimes, however, the sound of my own foot-falls on the gravel becomes an unpleasant noise that I prefer not to hear. So it was one June day, as I proceeded along a small, gated gravel road here on Foley Ridge in the Cascades.

I'd been walking along the vegetated median for only a few minutes when suddenly, only fifteen or twenty feet ahead of me, a chunky brownish bird erupted into flight and quickly disappeared farther ahead into the roadside brush. It was a mountain quail! Quails are birds of open, sunny areas, and I seldom see them here because most of the ridge is heavily forested. But there are a few areas which were logged in the early 1990s where there is still enough open space among the young trees that grass can grow and provide suitable habitat for the quail. And, of course, they find that same habitat along the edges of many forest roads.

Although I didn't get a good look at the bird that flew up, I knew from its "chunkiness" and relatively short, broad wings—as well as the short distance it flew at only a few feet from the ground—that it was a *gallinaceous* bird related to chickens and pheasants. These birds have very stout legs—since they spend most of their time running along the ground—and wings that are capable of flight, but not for very long distances. And the only gallinaceous bird of that size that is native to the West Cascades is the mountain quail.

I don't quite know why, but just after I came upon the quail, I stepped off the median and onto the left gravel track. A moment later, as I passed the spot from which the bird had flown, something caught my eye and I found myself looking down at a most curious sight. There, in a perfect circle maybe six or eight inches across were a couple dozen or more shiny, black balls about an eighth of an inch across. I first thought it was the very fresh scat or droppings of some animal, perhaps even the quail.

I squatted down for a closer look. Attached to each pair of little black spheres was a barely visible ball of beige and brown fluff. Here was an entire family of very young quail—only a day or two old at the most—sitting absolutely motionless on the ground with their shiny black eyes looking up at me!

I quickly decided to move on, so I wouldn't disturb or frighten them anymore than I already had. My mouth was agape as I continued walking and tried to comprehend what I'd just seen—and how close I'd come to stepping on the chicks, had I not veered off the median and onto the gravel only moments before.

Unlike many other birds whose young are nearly naked and helpless upon hatching, gallinaceous birds have what are called *precocious* young that are born with a thick layer of down and are able to run around and find their own food as soon as their fluff dries after hatching. But they still need the protection of a mother, and presumably some instruction from her about what is good to eat and what is not. Like all young, they need to rest, too, now and again. And that's just what they were apparently doing—snuggled all around the body of their crouching mother—when I arrived unexpectedly and their mother took flight.

The chicks responded instinctively by "freezing" and counted on their lack of movement and superb camouflage to keep from being noticed by me, their potential predator. Had they closed their eyes, too, I likely would have walked right on by. Instead, my attention was drawn to those eyes and I was treated to one of the most surprising and charming sights I've ever seen.

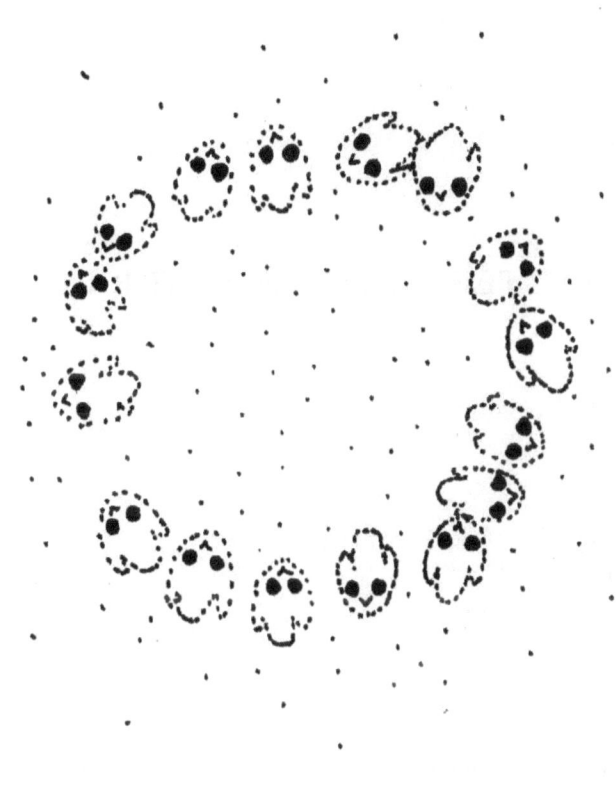

"The View from Above"
(Original sketch, June 2010)

A LETTER TO THE FOREST RANGER

17 April 2008

Head Ranger, McKenzie River Ranger District
Willamette National Forest
McKenzie Bridge, Oregon

Dear Ranger:

Because of the unusually deep and long-lasting snowpack this past winter, the road up Foley Ridge was closed for a record 15 weeks—since the last week of December 2007—so we animals at last had the place all to ourselves. Just a few days ago, however, we finally heard the dreaded sound of an axe biting into the trunk of a fallen tree that was still blocking the now nearly snow-free road near milepost one, and then the engine of a motorized vehicle making its way up the ridge.

It's true that, because of so much snow, there were many hardships for some of us who call the ridge our home. But those hardships were more than offset by the return of peace and tranquility to the ridge, in the absence of motorized vehicles and their sometimes ill-behaved occupants. Don't get us wrong—we have nothing against human beings *per se*. It's just that we abhor the contraptions in which most of them transport themselves, and the lack of consideration some of them show when visiting our home.

First of all, there's the noise. Most of the sounds we hear all day are pleasant—our bird friends singing, the wind in the trees, a tumbling brook. But suddenly, we hear in the distance a grumbling pick-up truck, or even a relatively quiet Prius coming around the bend, and BAM! the silence is broken.

Then, there is the aesthetic issue. After seeing nothing but trees and ferns and clouds for hour after hour, it's always a bit of a shock to glimpse a big plastic and metal box atop four or more rubber wheels moving through what we call our *Lebensraum* or "living room." In the old days, the light-green vehicles of the Forest Service weren't too bad, but these days, more often than not, most of the visitors' vehicles we see are painted garish colors like blue and red and even silver. We just don't understand this desire to "stand out" rather than "blend in" like the rest of us do. It's like seeing a discarded beer bottle alongside the road—it distracts our attention from the natural beauty that surrounds us the rest of the time.

Finally, there is the smell that many vehicles leave behind them, especially those awful diesel-powered pick-up trucks. For many minutes after they pass, their foul-smelling exhaust lingers in the otherwise pristine woodlands that line the roads along which these vehicles travel. The stench eventually dissipates, but (cough-cough!) we would prefer not to be subjected to it in the first place.

Another benefit of the long road closure was that no new roadside trash appeared in nearly four months! We really appreciate that. And we weren't startled from our afternoon naps by the sound of target shooters. Nor were we bothered by poachers—who most winters take quite a toll among us, especially on the deer.

Considering how often humans frequent the ridge during the rest of the year, it's amazing that no one visited during the snow—except for Whitey. He came up every week, whether it was snowing or raining, or cloudy or sunny. For some reason, he doesn't seem to need a motorized vehicle to visit the ridge—at least we never see him get into or out of one. And even though he is a two-legged animal, we like having him around because he's always quiet; he never leaves empty shotgun shells or beverage bottles or other trash in our living room; and he blends in nicely with the forest—except for that red backpack he carries. But as you humans say, "Nobody is perfect!"

Again, it was a wonderful winter on the ridge. And we're looking forward to a pleasant summer. But please understand that we won't be truly happy again until the next time the road is closed by snow.

Sincerely,

The wildlife of Foley Ridge

P.S. A special thanks to our friend Whitey for helping us to write this letter.

(Originally written in 2008, this letter "joined" the essay collection in 2010; hence, its inclusion in this volume of essays written between 2009 and 2011.)

HAMMOCK TIME

IT'S LATE AFTERNOON ON A SPLENDID SUMMER DAY here in the West Cascades. The temperature is about 80 degrees, with relative humidity maybe 30 or 40 percent, and a good up-ridge breeze is blowing. A perfect day for hiking! Or simply lying happily in my hammock.

In fact, I've spent most of the day doing just that. Unlike the other days of the week, when I have a long list of tasks to accomplish—some of which invariably remain still undone at day's end—my Thursday sabbaths have just one goal in mind, and that is to relax. That's an easy thing to do when one really puts one's mind to it.

"Relax" can mean wandering aimlessly through the forest, stopping and going when I feel like it—or sitting in the shade in the soft moss, as I am now, with my back against a tree. But my favorite way to relax is to lie in my hammock, asleep or awake. There is something about the way a little nylon hammock embraces one that is the sweetest of sensations.

I carry my green hammock with me whenever I go to the woods. It weighs only a few ounces and rolls up into a tiny, fist-sized package which fits perfectly into the lower side pocket of my Kelty pack. I've had it at least thirty years and I believe I originally purchased it at an Army Surplus store in Lancaster, Pennsylvania.

When it's time to string up the hammock, I look for two trees with trunks 6-18 inches in diameter and spaced eight to ten or so feet apart. I loop the braided yellow nylon cord at one end of the hammock around the trunk and loop it back through the steel ring to which the hammock's nylon mesh is attached. I then make a special knot—a slip knot that I invented that can be "locked"—both to ensure the knot doesn't come undone while I'm in the hammock (spilling me onto the ground), and to make it easy to undo when it's time to take the hammock down. After securing both ends, I straddle the somewhat drooping center of the hammock, and gently lower myself into it. (This action always produces a contented smile.)

I use my hammock especially in the summer—when there's no need to keep my back or buttocks next to the ground or a tree to preserve body heat—as I'm completely exposed to the ambient air once I'm in the hammock. And even on very warm days, I always wear socks, pants, and a shirt when lying in it, as I find the thin nylon mesh uncomfortable against my bare skin. One of the advantages of being in the hammock during the warm season is that, being off the ground, it gets me up where the cooling breeze can reach all sides of me. Another advantage of being up in the air is that I'm out of reach of ants, which can be pesky during the summer.

A third and very important advantage of the hammock is security. Ever since the frightful cougar attack of January 2001, I have been far more attentive to my personal safety when in the woods. Because cougars almost always attack from behind, and go for the neck of their prey, I am careful to have my back against a tree when seated on the ground, and I carry a frame pack that rides high enough on my back to conceal my neck. "Looking big" helps, too. When I'm lying in my hammock, not only is my neck facing the ground—making it inaccessible to a predator—but I also create a big and unfamiliar "package" to a potential predator, strung between two trees as I am. In short, I feel that my hammock provides me with complete security. I'm higher off the ground, too, which gives me a better view of the surrounding landscape and any large animals that might be lurking among the ferns.

So what do I "do" once I'm comfortably settled in my hammock? Well, it affords a great view up into the forest canopy, where I can see the treetops swaying in the breeze and the lovely sky beyond. And I can watch as the sun appears to move through the canopy, as the earth turns on its axis. It's always a delight, too, to gaze up into all that back-lit foliage—both needle-leafed and broad-leafed—and see the many beautiful patterns created by the incoming light.

Of course, Hammock Time is nearly synonymous with Nap Time, too. Some days, I just doze off and on—not really wanting to close my eyes for too long and possibly miss out on something that happens in the forest. But other days, I've slept for as much as an hour or more, and hammock sleeps are bliss-filled beyond belief, as one's body is supported in a completely different manner than it is in a bed or on the ground.

Over the years, I've come to use the term "hammock time" in a more figurative sense, too. When I talk about landscaping with native plants and creating landscapes where nature will do most of the work *for* us, I often mention that this gives us more hammock time—i.e., more time to relax and simply enjoy our time on the planet, instead of constantly going down our lists and getting through our over-scheduled days.

More than a decade ago, my brother Scot sent me a small package from his home in upstate New York, and I opened it to find his beloved little white nylon hammock—a sister to my own green one—which he had decided he no longer wanted. So now, when I bring a visitor with me to the woods, I always bring my second hammock so my visitor can enjoy hammock time together with me—each of us in our respective hammocks, of course. For some people, it's the first time they've ever been in a hammock. And the question they always ask me is, "Where can I get one of these?"

DEER CROSSING

WHEN I HEAD TO THE WEST CASCADES for some serious peace-and-quiet, I typically have my breakfast somewhere up on the ridge, away from the McKenzie River valley and its traffic noise. But today, after a brief meeting with a Forest Service fish biologist at the Ranger Station, I chose instead to walk just a quarter of a mile or so up the riverside hiking trail, to enjoy my breakfast at my usual *supper* spot that I call Table Rock.

I'm right down by the water, with my feet only inches from it at this season, and I set my meal atop a bushel-basket-size, flat-topped, moss-covered boulder. Years ago, when I was first looking for the ideal spot along this part of the river to have my evening meal, I chose this stretch of relatively quiet water that separates two much livelier and louder stretches. One reason is there is less river noise here, so it's easier to hear other natural sounds. And, fortunately, I'm also far enough from the highway that only the very loudest vehicles are audible.

A second reason is because there are two enormous boulders just off-shore here, the mossy tops of which barely stick out of the water in summer. These serve as "stepping boulders" to get me easily to deep water where I often take a pre-prandial dip. Yes, the McKenzie is a cold, spring-fed river, reaching a *maximum* temperature just east of McKenzie Bridge in late summer of 53 degrees Fahrenheit, and a minimum in winter about 42 degrees. But the experience is always revivifying, and I seldom stay in for more than ten or twenty seconds.

On this overcast and cool day, I chose not to take a dip, but instead opened my pack immediately after arriving, and took out my jar of müesli—oats, yogurt, milk, honey, cinnamon, salt . . . and today, fresh red raspberries—and my spoon, and began my first course. (Second course is a small jar of orange juice; third is a cup of Earl Grey tea from my trusty thermos.) The view from Table Rock includes the river, of course—which here is some one hundred feet across—and then an impressive forest of tall red- and incense-cedars and Douglas-firs on the north bank.

Occasionally, a dipper will fly by. It's a gray, robin-sized songbird that lives its entire life along fast-flowing mountain streams and rivers, and eats a variety of aquatic critters that it finds while alternately swimming and walking (yes!) underwater. Now and then, I see mergansers—fast-flying ducks that, while they're floating along on the river's surface, occasionally dive underwater to feed on fish. Once in a while, a great blue heron flies past, and in summer, fish-eating osprey frequently fly by overhead. One time, I even saw from here a mink scampering among the rocks on the far bank!

But this morning, as I mused over my müesli, I looked up to see something I had never seen before: Not twenty feet away, two *deer heads* were floating by! Initially, I thought that a poacher just upriver a ways had illegally killed two deer, then cut off the deers' heads and tossed them in the river, so he could hide the animals' bodies in the trunk of his car. But I very quickly realized that the two dead deers' *heads* were in fact still attached to two very alive deers' *bodies* that were "jogging" underwater in the swift current.

By the time the two deer neared the shore, they had been carried just a short distance downstream from where I was sitting. The doe reached shallow water first, and stood up, staring in my direction—where I sat motionless. She clearly saw me, but didn't know quite what to make of me, except that I didn't appear dangerous.

While she stood knee-deep in the shallows, her wet fur matted and dripping after the river crossing, her half-grown fawn struggled to get around some waterlogged and submerged branches before joining her. The two of them then stood there for ten or twenty seconds and quietly stared at me, before slowly making their way to the bank and disappearing into the woods.

I am aware, of course, that all the large mammals native to this area—black bear, Roosevelt elk, and cougar, as well as blacktail deer—are capable swimmers. Nonetheless, the sight of the two heads floating by—with long brown ears and big shiny, black eyes—certainly made me stop chewing my müesli for a few moments!

THE DAY-NEST

AN IMPORTANT PART of enjoying a visit to The Woods—or anywhere else outdoors where one might go to seek solitude and appreciate the wonders of wild places—is taking the time to sit still and let the site's peacefulness flow into you. One of the reasons relatively few people do this is that they see "woods time" as "recreation time." To them, that means nearly constant physical activity, whether hiking on a trail, actively looking for birds, or reaching the top of the mountain by lunchtime.

A second reason, I believe, is that most people simply don't know *how* to make themselves truly comfortable when away from their plush, heated (and now, even *cooled*) car seats, their La-Z-Boy recliners, and the oversized and overstuffed mattresses on which they sleep. Some outdoor enthusiasts have even taken to carrying portable chairs with them when they go outside, or at the very least an inflatable sit-upon.

I have finally come to the conclusion that I need to explain how to construct what I call a "day-nest"—which is just a temporary ground-level seat from which one can enjoy one's surroundings in total comfort. Like all good things these days, a day-nest is ideally constructed from locally available, organically-grown, and recyclable materials. For example, the day-nest I am sitting in to write this essay is composed of about a dozen Douglas-fir boughs, each about two feet long, that I snapped off from the lower branches of the ten-year-old fir trees that surround me. (Yes, it's okay to do this, in my opinion, when away from trails, as I am, where others are unlikely to follow anytime soon. And within a few years, the lower branches of these young firs will die anyway, as they become shaded out from the developing tree canopy above.)

I've placed the boughs in a roughly oval area, with their butt (broken) ends facing outward, and the soft tips facing the center, where I'm sitting. By choosing to use a conifer for my day-nest, I also know that it will smell oh-so-good, both from the sap at the snapped-off ends, as well as from the needles that are gently crushed as I snuggle into my nest. Other appropriate and readily available materials in western Oregon—although not as fluffy as fir boughs—are Pacific sword-fern fronds, the boughs of both western hemlock and western red-cedar, and the luxuriant epiphytic mosses that often festoon the easily-reached branches of shrub-like vine maples in local forests.

Besides being constructed of clean and comfortable materials—that will also keep your clothes or body from contact with moist ground during the wet season—some of the other attributes of the perfect day-nest include:

- A slightly concave spot—or depression—where one's derrière will be
- Something behind the day-nest to afford a feeling of security, so one cannot be "surprised" from behind (this might be a boulder, a stump, a tree trunk, or a shrub)
- A nice view, either off into the surrounding forest's undercanopy, down into a valley, up a stream, across a meadow, etc.
- A somewhat inclined area behind the concave spot onto which one might easily lower one's back to take a nap—or to look up into the sky and watch the clouds go by, or up into the forest canopy and watch the tree-tops sway in the breeze

If it's a wet day, it's nice to place your day-nest at the base of a young conifer or a well-branched shrub, so an umbrella—one of Whitey's *Ten Essentials* when visiting the woods—can be positioned directly above you among the overhead branches, to keep you dry. I also carry with me year-round a small (a foot square or so), half-inch thick insulite pad (or "sit-upon") and a forest-green wool blanket—both of which ameliorate my day-nest comfort considerably when it's wet or cold.

Although some people are accustomed to sitting on logs or on stumps when taking a rest while out-of-doors, those options just aren't the same as a day-nest. For one thing, those seats are *hard*, compared to the ground. And their elevated position is too similar to a chair to provide the comfort—and the possibility of reclining—that a day-nest on the ground does. Having taught field classes for many years for students of all ages—including quite a few over age 70—I am aware that getting down to the ground and then up *off* the ground again can be more difficult for some older folks. But you just need to know how to do it: Once down, instead of trying to push off the ground and stand straight up, simply roll onto your side, then arise, one body segment at a time—first torso, then hips, then legs—or ask someone for a little help. I realize, too, that some older people just don't like sitting on the ground, period—it's simply an uncomfortable position. So save the logs and stumps for *them*.

As for me, even though I'm nearing the end of my sixth decade, I spend as much time as possible when out-of-doors in day-nests of my own creation, some of them in my favorite spots re-used (and freshened up with just-picked boughs) dozens of times over the years. Many of our closest simian relatives—for example, chimpanzees and gorillas—make new day-nests daily, where they either nap or just rest between foraging trips.

The perfect day-nest is simply a comfortable and secure spot—slightly improved with appropriate vegetation—in which to happily while away some of one's brief time on the planet.

A TYPICAL UPRIVER THURSDAY
In Lines of Only Three Syllables

Good night's sleep
A new day
Rise and shine
Sky looks clear
Put clothes on
Go downstairs
Wash my face
Boil water
Let tea steep
Add honey
Fill thermos
Make breakfast
(see below)
Prepare lunch
Pack backpack
Feed chickens
Check rain-gauge
Sweep terrace
Put pack on
Hiking stick
Close the door
Sun's just up
Spencer Butte
Catches rays
Walk to bus
Eighty-two

Dollar coins
(three of them,
for all day!)
Ride to town
Change buses
Ninety-one
Up-river!
Sixty miles
Off the bus
In the woods
Down the road
Up the hill
Breakfast spot
Madrone Bluff
A warm sun
Cold müesli
Orange juice
Earl Grey tea
Make day-nest
(fresh fir boughs)
Take a nap
Wake back up
Stare at sky
Watch the trees
Smell the air
Touch the moss
Hear the stream
Taste some snow
Tree shadow
No more sun
Cooling down
Time to move
Off I go
See kinglets
(golden-crowned)
Down the hill
Cross the road
Then the creek
(Two Trout Creek,
 North Fork here)
Rain-swollen
Careful, boy
Up the slope

Cathedral!
(tall, old trees)
Up the hill
Zig-zag trail
Up on top
Much more snow
Find a spot
This one's great
New day-nest
(more fir boughs)
Face the sun
Lunch-time yet?
No, not quite
Write letter
Lunch-time now!
Good sandwich
(cheese and friends)
Crunchy chips
Blackberries
Choc-o-late
Raven's call
Then gray jay
Chickadee
Clouds move in
Time to go
Head downhill
Bye, Two Trout!
Back to road
Then highway
Other side
River trail
Supper spot
High water
New day-nest
This one moss
Take off pack
Light candle
Writing time
Then supper
Small sandwich
S'more chips
Carrot cake
Last of tea

Blow out light
Fond farewell
Catch the bus
Ninety-one
Down-river!
Back to town
Change buses
Eighty-one
Home Sweet Home
Turn on heat
Make om'let
Have a beer
(Rolling Rock)
And dessert
(with ice cream)
Brush my teeth
Turn off heat
Back to bed
All is well
What a day!

A RECORD IS (QUIETLY) BROKEN
Aural Snapshot No. 14

THE STORM THAT MOVED IN OFF THE PACIFIC yesterday and began to peter out during the night left about ten inches of fresh snow here on the ridge. It's late forenoon now, and although the occasional passing cloud still spits out a few snow pellets that plink when they hit my nylon backpack lying next to me, the skies have been mostly sunny for more than an hour. And there's nothing quite like the hour or two after a good snowfall—before birds and other creatures have become active again—to just sit and listen to The Great Quiet.

So it is, here at what I call Nighthawk Knob, a slight eminence in a stand of twenty-year-old Douglas-firs and western white pines that were planted after this area was logged around 1990. I've come to this spot because, even when the sun is about as low in the sky as it can get during the entire year—the winter solstice was just a few days ago—I'm far enough away from the tall uncut forest to the south, that the sun's rays can still reach over those treetops to fall on me and warm me on this otherwise cold day.

I've recorded more than a half-dozen aural snapshots in this vicinity before—several of them under similar circumstances, just after a good snowfall and when there is no wind—so it will be interesting to see how this one compares. For sixty consecutive minutes, from noon until one o'clock, I shall note every sound I hear, and whether the sound occurs only once during that minute, or is repetitive or constant.

*　　　*　　　*　　　*　　　*

The results are in. As the sun grew ever-stronger midday and the temperature rose to nearly 40 degrees, snow began to melt and fall from the branches of nearby conifers, creating a gentle sound that continued during most of the hour—a sound that I therefore chose not to include in my recording. And since I'd just finished a very late breakfast about a half-hour before beginning to record, my tummy was somewhat talkative, too, as I'd had nothing to eat since last evening. So I discounted this sound, as well, and focused instead on whatever else I could hear.

Over the years of doing these snapshots, I've occasionally had single minutes—sometimes even two or three in a row, and one time *nine* consecutive minutes—when I heard absolutely nothing. But never before did I experience so many cumulative minutes of silence as I just did this past hour. There were two periods of single-minute silence; one that was two minutes long; three four minutes long; and two that were six consecutive minutes in duration. That's a total of twenty-eight minutes— nearly a half-hour—of blissful silence. (My previous record, on 16 February 2006, was a total of twenty-six minutes.)

Of course, a day here in the West Cascades would not be "complete" without the noise of commercial jets—which pollutes the acoustical environment here, on average, for twenty-four minutes of every hour. Interestingly, today was a perfectly average day with exactly twenty-four minutes of jet noise.

That covers fifty-two of the sixty minutes so far: twenty-eight quiet ones and twenty-four filled with jet noise. What about the other eight? Unlike most every other aural snapshot I've done—where bird and insect sounds dominate the hour, even in winter—not a single insect was heard during the past hour, and very few birds. Six of the remaining eight minutes included the sound of a gray jay; one included both a raven cawing as it flew overhead and a gray jay nearby; and one minute included one raven call and no other sound.

At the end of the hour, as I tallied up the minutes and the sounds and realized that my old record for minutes of silence had been broken, I wanted to let out a jubilant whoop—but, of course, that would have been completely out of line. Instead, I simply broke into a broad smile and cheered mutely to myself.

TRACKS IN THE SNOW

WE HAD JUST FINISHED OUR CLASS in animal tracking, and were eager to put our new skills to use. So when we heard that there was fresh snow at fairly low elevation in the West Cascades, we grabbed our daypacks and hopped the bus to the McKenzie River Ranger Station about sixty miles east of Eugene.

Along the way, we talked about what kinds of tracks we might see during the day—from mouse and grouse, to elk and cougar—but we all agreed not to have any expectations that might not be met. That way, we could be assured of a satisfying day, regardless of what kinds of tracks we encountered.

Less than a hundred feet east of the ranger station, we came upon our first set of tracks, and they were *huge*. What a way to start the day! Although we had no way to measure them, each one was about a foot long, and fairly broad. The tracks were really fresh and headed east along the narrow utility-line corridor. Many large animals follow forest trails and roads made by humans, just because they are easy alternatives to getting around in the often dense undergrowth of western Oregon forests.

The only animal we could think of with tracks that big was a bear. Most people think that all bears hibernate in the winter, but our instructor taught us that, in areas like this with mild winters, a bear might curl up under a log or in a hollow tree and take an extended snooze or two, but it never truly hibernates as it would in colder areas. Our excitement level was high as we continued along the utility corridor.

Soon we saw our next set of tracks. They were in groups of four, and the groups were about a foot apart. Hmm. Definitely a mammal, we agreed, and one that *hopped* rather than walked left-right-left-right. It looked too big for a chipmunk—and anyway, chipmunks *do* hibernate at that elevation (about 1,500 feet). We finally decided that it was probably a chickaree, a small native squirrel that is very common in conifer forests and active all winter long.

A little farther along, just before we got to a small forest road, we encountered another set of tracks. This animal had clearly walked left-right-left-right and each track consisted of two oval-shaped prints side-by-side that were pointed at one end and about three inches long. We knew it must be a large mammal—the question was which one? Someone suggested Roosevelt elk. But elk are really big animals with much larger tracks than these—five inches or more in length—and they are double ovals that are *rounded* at both ends, not pointed at one end like these tracks. That meant that they must have been made by a blacktail deer, the only other large mammal in this area with a so-called cloven hoof that divides each track into two parts.

We were still following the huge tracks we'd first encountered back near the ranger station. When we reached the small forest road, they headed to the right and up the hill, following the road. The animal that made them was definitely walking left-right-left-right—large animals rarely hop, except for short distances (e.g., deer)—but we couldn't figure out what its fore-paw tracks looked like because, as the animal moved along, its hind-paws were evidently placed in the same spots as the fore-paws, thus obliterating the fore-paw tracks. We continued to scratch our heads over this one.

Then, a new set of tracks crossed the road and abruptly disappeared beside a roadside log. These were little depressions in the snow—created by the entire body of a small animal—rather than actual tracks or footprints. Each one was maybe an inch across and a half-inch deep, and they were less than six inches apart and in a straight line. Too small for a chipmunk's body, we thought—and we reminded ourselves once again that chipmunks would be hibernating anyway. So we decided it must have been some kind of vole or mouse that briefly hopped across the surface of the snow before reaching the log where it burrowed back down to the ground.

Suddenly, after following the forest road for a mile or so, the huge tracks turned and headed into a stand of old trees. Just before leaving the road, one of us noticed an especially clear track in which we could see what almost appeared to be rows of small depressions, as if the paw of the animal, instead of being flat, was covered with little bumps. We agreed that this would probably ensure better traction in snow, so the animal could get around easily in winter.

As we made our way through the forest—still following the big tracks—we encountered another set of deer tracks, as well as several more sets of chickaree tracks. Still no grouse. Well, we hadn't wanted to have any expectations, but we were nevertheless hoping we might cross paths with a grouse—a mostly ground-dwelling, pheasant-like bird that is common in these forests. But grouse typically seek cover during and just after snowfalls, so maybe they were still inside one of the dense rhododendron thickets we passed, where they would be somewhat protected.

The big tracks ascended a small hill, following what appeared to be a fairly well used animal trail. When we came out of the woods into a clearing, the snow was much deeper and softer than it had been below, and the tracks were less well defined—yet still easy to follow due to their size.

After crossing through a stand of young trees, we reached another small forest road where we noticed, in addition to the big tracks, a set of tracks in a mostly straight line that resembled dimples in the snow, and were perhaps two to three inches in diameter. At first, we thought they were made by another mouse—except they were more than 18 inches apart from each other, farther than a mouse could hop in deep, soft snow, and twice as big as the earlier mouse "depressions" had been. We finally figured out that they were *deer* tracks that had been made before the snow stopped falling, and then were partly filled with additional snow that fell after the deer had passed through that area.

We were still following the big tracks when, as we approached a cluster of small madrone trees, the young woman at the head of our group gave us the signal to freeze where we were and be completely silent. Apparently, she had finally sighted the animal whose tracks we had been following for the past hour. When she turned around, we could see that she was smiling. Then, putting her index finger to her lips, to ensure that we kept quiet, she motioned for the rest of us to come join her just behind the madrones.

We excitedly made our way up to the little rise and, reaching it, we looked down to see—curled up and asleep in the sunshine—not a fat Oregon black bear after all, but our animal tracking instructor, Whitey! Beside him were his big, knobby-soled Sorel Caribou winter boots, which he'd shed just before settling down to take a nap.

Here, we had discovered Whitey's secret place where he goes on pleasant winter days to just enjoy the solitude. With smiles all around, we quietly— so we didn't disturb Whitey—shook each other's hands and patted one another's shoulders, then returned the way we had come. What a great day we'd had!

THE HANDSOME SAILOR

D URING MY PERIPATETIC YEARS—the decade after I graduated from Penn State—I lived in five countries and eight cities before settling down in Eugene, Oregon. One of my homes was in Nantes, France—a bustling seaport city about thirty miles up the Loire River from the Atlantic Ocean. I got to know countless people during my year in Nantes, from colleagues at the Municipal Parks Department where I worked, to the policemen directing traffic whom I passed daily on my bicycle, to students at the university cafeteria where I ate my lunches and dinners.

One of my friends was a twenty-ish, cherub-cheeked little ball of energy named Jean-Louis. We went to movies together, had long discussions in cafés with our other friends, and listened to music at the relatively posh dormitory where we both lived. One evening, Jean-Louis suggested we go down to the docks and see what we might find, and soon we were carousing with half a dozen young sailors whose ship was in port for a day or two.

Most of the sailors—from Egypt, Sri Lanka, Saudi Arabia, and Chile—were unremarkable in appearance and had limited language skills. One young man from Chile, however, was the exception. "Jaime" was exceedingly handsome, solidly built, spoke very good English, and seemed to have had a much more privileged upbringing than his sailor buddies. Wherever we went, Jaime was the center of attention, and the other sailors clustered around him, literally looking up to his Adonis-like frame, as if in the company of royalty.

During the course of the evening, the conversation within the group was amusing, as no one could speak directly to more than one or two of the others in the group. So, for example, if Jean-Louis wanted to share something with everyone, he would say it to me in French. I'd then translate it to English for Jaime, who'd say it in Spanish to a fellow Chilean who knew a little Arabic, and so forth.

The night wore on and just before heading back to the dormitory I took a photo of all my new sailor-friends, and exchanged addresses with Jaime— promising to send one another a postcard or two. But he and I soon lost track of each other, as our lives went in different directions on opposite sides of the globe.

I hadn't thought of Jaime in many years until I recently read Herman Melville's *Billy Budd—Sailor* for the first time. In the book's opening paragraph, Melville describes a scene that seemed incredibly familiar to me:

> *"In the time before steamships, or then more frequently than now, a stroller along the docks of any considerable seaport would occasionally have his attention arrested by a group of bronzed mariners . . . in holiday attire, ashore on liberty. In certain instances, they would flank, or like a bodyguard quite surround, some superior figure of their own class, moving along with them like Aldebaran among the lesser lights of his constellation. That signal object was the 'Handsome Sailor' . . . . With no perceptible trace of the vainglorious about him, rather with the offhand unaffectedness of natural regality, he seemed to accept the spontaneous homage of his shipmates."*

How extraördinary! I promptly got out my 1974 journal and read about the November night I met Jaime. His full name, it turned out, was Jaime Allende (high-may eye-YENN-day)—and suddenly the memories came flooding back. I distinctly recall Jaime winking at me, as he wrote down his name and address, and telling me that he had a very famous uncle in Chile with the same last name. At the time, that meant nothing to me. But now, decades later—after my interest in and knowledge of world history and politics finally blossomed—I realized, to my astonishment, that I evidently spent one very memorable night of my life with none other than the nephew of former Chilean president, Salvador Allende.

It was not uncommon, in years past, for certain well-to-do families to send off their sons to "sail the seven seas" and, along the way, learn something about themselves and about the rest of the world. So it was that the wealthy Allende family apparently sent Jaime off to see the world and, in the distant

French seaport of Nantes, to make the acquaintance of a young man from Pennsylvania who was on his own voyage of self-discovery.

A GIFT FROM THE CLASS OF 2008

I HAVE A GOOD TIME WITH MY STUDENTS in the Trees Across Oregon class I teach at the University of Oregon. Although we spend only ten weeks together, it's long enough for us to get to know each other and for a degree of fondness to develop among us. Although my fondness for them is seldom expressed in words, they soon learn from my actions that I care about them very much, indeed.

Like most relationships, ours starts out slowly. I'm careful for the first week of class not to make too many jokes, because I know that the response of most of the students that early in the term would be tepid, at best. But by the second or third week, we've already gotten to know each other much better, and the friendly banter begins to flow in both directions.

When I show slides the fourth week of the class about my graduate school research involving whitebark pine in Oregon's High Cascades—during the late 1970s—they are clearly amused by some of the slides of a very young Whitey and fascinated by the stories I tell them of living alone in a tent for the better part of two years at an elevation of nearly 8,000 feet on Bachelor Butte, Oregon. Immediately following the lecture, I pull out several plates of oatmeal-and-pine-nut cookies from behind the lectern—since I talk about pine nuts (or seeds) during the slides—and you should see their faces light up! They're always grateful to me for having baked cookies for all 66 of them, and the class often breaks out in spontaneous applause at that moment.

The last day of the term, I have ended my lecture for the past several years with a series of fourteen of my finest slides of Oregon's trees and forests, accompanied by the Beatles singing *Because* ("Because the world is round, it turns me on; because the wind is high, it blows my mind; because the sky is blue, it makes me cry. . . ."). It's a bittersweet moment because we all realize that our time together is about to end—and we don't want it to.

One year, just before the beginning of the last class, one of my young male students came into the room and announced to me and to anyone else within earshot, "This is a kind of sad day because it's the last day of Trees Across Oregon." I couldn't have agreed more, but I try to keep my emotions in check, at least in the classroom.

The first week of June 2008, however, something happened that nearly made me completely "lose it" right there in front of everyone. It was a warm spring day and the energy level was even higher than usual. All 66 students had taken their seats for the final, and I had at last gotten them to settle down and be quiet, so I could pass out the exams.

Although I have two teaching assistants for the course, I prefer on the day of the final to walk up and down each row of chairs myself and personally hand the students their exams, while looking into their eyes and saying their names. It's my way of showing them that I care about them, and saying farewell.

As I was walking down the first row, Laura—one of my best students that year, and a bit of an extrovert—asked me in a voice loud enough for everyone to hear, "Is it okay, Whitey, if we give you something?" I smiled at her as I continued to hand out the exams, and said, "I suppose so."

She looked over at some of her friends and, as if on cue, they began to applaud. Then everyone else in the classroom joined in. I didn't have time to think about what to say or do, and I just turned bright red with embarrassment as students said, "Great class, Whitey!" "It was awesome!" and the like.

Over the years, my students have given me many wonderful gifts, most of them the intangible kind. But the gift of applause, accompanied by accolades for my course—while I was handing out their final exams, no less—was the best gift I have ever received.

SALVAGING THE DAY

I AWOKE WITH A START. Oh, no—it was already light outside! What had happened? At this time of year, it's always dark when I get up on Thursdays, my special day every week that I get to spend alone in the woods.

I glanced at my watch and it was 7:50. WHAT?! I should have left the house by 7:45 in order to catch the bus up to the mountains in time! Then I looked at my clock radio, and realized that the alarm set for 6:35 hadn't gone off.

There was no way I could stay home—or even in town. Not only would I be disappointed in myself all day, but what if one of my friends or students saw me? Many people know that I'm out of town on Thursdays, and if I'm not, then something must be dreadfully wrong.

I lay in bed for another minute or two, just staring outside into the brightening sky and wondering what I could do. Then it struck me: I'd go instead to the "other" woods, the forested area of Spencer Butte Park on the south edge of Eugene. I hadn't been there since fall, and I knew a place where I could meet my two major objectives for Thursday by 1) not seeing or hearing anyone else all day, and 2) not being exposed to city noises like train horns, traffic, police sirens, and leaf blowers.

Without any further delay, I threw back my down comforter, got dressed, and headed downstairs to pack both my breakfast and my lunch before heading out. I decided to ride my bike to the trailhead just two miles away—rather than take the bus—so I could stick to back streets and not see, hear, or smell the bumper-to-bumper cars of commuters along the main streets.

It wasn't even nine o'clock yet when I locked my bike to a pole near the Martin Street trailhead, turned my back on the city, and headed into the woods. Just moments before disappearing beneath the tree canopy, though, my thoughts were interrupted by an unwanted noise one last time as the annoying fan of a heat-exchanger at a nearby dwelling started up.

But not one minute later, as I crossed the first wooden footbridge over the headwaters of Amazon Creek, I broke into a smile and immediately felt better when I realized that I'd finally left all city noises behind and I could hear only the blissful sounds of what I call natural silence. For the next half-hour that it took me to hike up to the junction with the main Ridgeline Trail, I heard only the call of a winter wren, a singing junco, and the gentle "good morning" of a solitary female jogger—the only person I met all day—as she passed me on the trail.

After crossing semi-rural Fox Hollow Road and seeing and hearing several motorized vehicles, I tucked back into the woods again, and followed the trail up past the Cascades Raptor Center where someone was pounding nails into a board. After another half-mile or so of uphill hiking, I looked off to the south, to a parcel of private land that had been logged five or ten years ago, where, in between light showers, the sun was shining.

So I left the maintained park trail and followed a deer trail up the gentle slope to the clearing where I soon found a pleasant grass-covered spot to unpack and sit down to enjoy my breakfast. In the distance, to the east, I could see the West Cascades—my usual Thursday destination—with snowy patches visible on the higher ridges. I sighed. But I fended off the feeling of disappointment. Today, I would simply be satisfied with the solitude of Spencer Butte rather than that of my accustomed Foley Ridge.

After breakfast, it began to sprinkle a bit. I repacked my things, walked a little farther south along the grass-covered former logging road, then turned back west and uphill through a lovely grove of Oregon white oaks, incense-cedars, and madrones, to return to parkland and the tall fir forest where I was anticipating spending the bulk of my day.

Less than 100 yards inside the forest, I arrived at this spot where I've come many times before. I selected two fir trunks about a dozen feet apart, stretched a cord between them, and then put up my tarp lean-to where I shall spend most of the rest of the day—which looks like it's going to be pretty wet. And a gentle ridge just to my north prevents any distant city noises from reaching me.

I am now perfectly situated—beneath my tarp and atop my foam sit-upon, with my legs wrapped in a wool blanket—to spend the day here, doing what needs to be done. That includes staring off into the ferns, listening to passing flocks of golden-crowned kinglets, eating, doing a little writing, and napping. These five "tasks" will together ensure that I'll return home later today completely refreshed, and confident that I successfully "salvaged" this day which, at its outset, seemed doomed to disappointment.

THE END OF WINTER

TODAY WAS MY FOURTH DAY of a six-day visit here on Oregon's central coast, where I've come for some extended peace-and-quiet before spring term begins at the university. Thanks to the moderating influence of the Pacific Ocean—the surf of which I hear constantly, either close-by when I'm along the littoral, or at a distance when in the spruce forests just inland—"winter" is only a relative term. It rarely brings snow, and seldom even brings heavy frost. What it does bring are long nights, periods of rain, and a conspicuous lack of the warmer seasons' birds and flowers.

The last time I visited—the second week of December—winter had not yet "officially" arrived, but it was "wintry" nonetheless. December is always the most difficult month for me to camp here, as I need to get into my tent around 5 p.m. when darkness falls, and don't go back outside again until after first light around 8 a.m. That makes *fifteen* hours of tent time which, even with a good imagination, plenty to do (read and write), and a candle for light, is a long time to be "inside" and unable to stand up or move around much.

But today is officially the last day of winter, and already it feels like spring. First light came around 7 a.m. and the sun didn't set into the blue Pacific until after 7 p.m. Only *twelve* hours to spend inside my tent, yay!

In anticipation of the vernal equinox tomorrow, there were already today "signs of spring" wherever I went. Just south of Bob Creek—which is not far from my campsite—I found hundreds of fragrant white narcissus in bloom in the seaside meadows. These flowers are native to Europe, but some bulbs likely found their way here many years ago, when the owners of private land just across the highway tossed them here along with other garden refuse, and the narcissus settled into their new home quite nicely.

About a mile south of there, just after leaving the relatively noisy coast highway and turning onto peaceful Tenmile Creek Road, I came upon a south-facing cut-bank just covered with the happy faces of yellow wood violets. And not much farther along, the first shin-high heads of the native coltsfoot were in subtly fragrant bloom in the roadside gravel, a favorite place for this plant.

After enjoying my lunch under a massive Sitka spruce tree, with a view out across a grassy meadow to Tenmile Creek, I headed back to the little forest road. Along the way, what should I see among the huge sword ferns, nestled atop the moss and fallen spruce needles, but a half-grown rough-skinned newt, curled into an S shape and completely immobile. As soon as the days warm up—today was unseasonably cool, with a high only in the 40s—this little guy will be a bit livelier, I'm sure.

Back by the road, I found a small, south-facing clearing where I basked in the sunshine for the better part of an hour, happy that the sun is much higher and stronger than it was three months ago at the winter solstice.

Then it was time to return to the highway and make my way back north to my campsite. Along the way, I passed a patch of bright yellow skunk cabbage—another harbinger of spring here on the coast—and lowered my nose to the just-emerging foliage of a thimbleberry plant, which is wonderfully fragrant, especially in the warm sunshine.

I generally eschew hiking along the shoulder of the coast highway, but along the stretch north of Tenmile Creek, I can't walk on the beach due to precipitous cliffs against which the surf crashes. Despite the traffic hurtling on by me, I see things along the way that help keep my spirits high. Today, it was the sight of a large bird soaring above the alder-cloaked hillsides just a bit inland: my first turkey vulture of 2011! Most of them overwinter in Mexico, then return here in late winter (that's today) and earliest spring—which is tomorrow!

Now that winter will be officially over, it won't be long before the first gray whales are sighted off-shore here again as they head back to spend the summer feeding off the coast of Alaska, after wintering in the warm lagoons of Baja California. And waves of songbirds will return, too, as insects—on which many of these birds feed—become more active and abundant again.

The "end" of winter isn't really noticeable as it blends into the beginning of spring. But for a *brief* moment tomorrow, the first day of spring, both the north and south poles of the earth will be equidistant from the sun—as they are at the autumnal equinox as well—and then the north pole will gradually and imperceptibly tilt more and more toward the sun until the first day of summer here in the northern hemisphere, when it begins to tilt back again. But most of us will by then be too distracted by the longer, warmer, and drier days to even notice.

A JOYFUL BUZZING

I T'S THURSDAY AND, AS USUAL, I've spent the day alone here in the West Cascades—except, of course, for all the other *non*-human beings with whom I share this area. Last night was cold and frosty, even back in town, but my day up here has been sunny and warm, with a very light breeze from the west.

I've spent the better part of the day—and I mean that quite literally—here at the base of Sixteen Madrones, my favorite "day-nest" from late fall until mid-spring. The rest of the year, this site just gets too hot for comfort on many days. And then there are the ants during the warm season, which are a nearly constant aggravation when one is sitting on the ground in open areas like this.

This patch of forest was logged in 1990, and one of the trees cut was a Pacific madrone which was then about a hundred years old, having germinated shortly after the last forest fire to burn through here around 1890. Following the logging, the area was "broadcast burned." That is, a controlled fire was sent across the entire site to prepare the area for replanting with, in this case, Douglas-firs and western white pines.

Because there was not much natural fuel to burn—branches, cones, and such—the fire was relatively cool. So although it burned the tops of shrubs and groundcovers and charred the stumps of cut trees, many of the plants, including this madrone, were able to resprout the following season. After several years, the madrone had developed sixteen new trunks around the perimeter of its old stump, and thus earned the name I gave to it sometime in the late 1990s.

Madrones are broad-leafed evergreen trees that lose all of their old leaves from the preceding year in mid-summer, just after the current year's leaves have fully developed. They bloom in mid-spring, producing showy clusters of small, milky-white flowers that, once they're dropped resemble (no kidding) miniature showerheads. When they are in bloom, they are visited and pollinated by a great variety of insects, as well as by hummingbirds.

After finishing my picnic lunch in early afternoon, I lay back on my blanket, stuffed my sweater under my head, and promptly fell asleep in the dappled shade here. It's been quite a busy week, with back-to-back all-day field trips with my Trees Across Oregon students last weekend, class on Monday, essays from last week that still needed to be graded, and then the midterm exam yesterday. So my "nap" was much needed, and it lasted for almost two hours!

When I awoke, I heard what sounded like a symphony going on just above me. Insects of every size were swarming around the madrone flowers, from the tiniest gnats to hover flies—bee imitators (that are actually flies) with fuzzy, striped abdomens—and the occasional bumblebee or butterfly. Except for the butterflies, each insect was humming a pitch appropriate to its size, so the gnats were the sopranos and the bumblebees the basses. Every few minutes, a male Anna's hummingbird flew into the madrone's canopy, adding his whirring and humming to the symphony. It was a joy to behold, and I lay here for the longest time just watching and listening, until the sun began to descend in the west and the pollinators sensed that their day's work was done and it was time to go home.

Before today, I usually associated the sound of buzzing and humming insects with something unpleasant—such as a mosquito intent on probing me with its blood-sucking proboscis. But from now on, I'll know that these sounds can also create *pleasant* sensations, thanks to my glorious afternoon "at the symphony" here at Sixteen Madrones.

A VISIT TO THE PALACE ENDS BADLY

IN PREPARATION FOR MY TRIP to visit Ecuador in late 1982, I wrote to Dr. Misael Acosta-Solís—one of the country's leading botanists—who subsequently invited me to visit him when I reached Quito. He also asked me to join him on a botanical excursion to the upper Amazon in eastern Ecuador. So I was most eager to meet this man, and to learn from him what I could about tropical forest biology.

My first two weeks in the country were spent just north of the port city of Guayaquil, where my friends Fran and Aaron worked for the Peace Corps just outside of Portoviejo. I then continued north by bus and by boat to the coastal city of Esmeraldas, before heading up to Quito, which is situated at an elevation of about 10,000 feet in the Andes Mountains.

There, I stayed with an American couple—friends of friends of mine at the University of Wisconsin, where I was in graduate school at the time—while I explored the Quito area. One of my first tasks was to meet Dr. Acosta-Solís, which turned out to be quite difficult. I stopped by his home, but he was away at the time. I telephoned him, only to receive no answer. Finally, I learned from his housekeeper that he was ill, and I received a note from him saying that he'd have to cancel our trip to the jungle.

I was deeply disappointed, but made arrangements to visit the area by myself. After an exhilarating week exploring the upper Amazon basin— where I traveled for the most part by motor-driven dug-out canoe—I returned to Quito, took a room in the rather shabby Hotel Hilton (no relation to the American hotel chain!), and telephoned Dr. Acosta-Solís again. He had recovered from his illness, and we finally got to meet each other. I spoke excitedly of what I'd seen in eastern Ecuador, and he was able to identify for me some of the plants I'd seen that were unfamiliar to me. Before I left his house, he gave me a beautifully printed invitation to attend a ceremony at the Palacio Legislativo, where he was to receive a medal of honor from the president.

I couldn't believe it. I was just a lowly, 30-year-old graduate student from the U.S., but here I was invited to rub elbows with some of Ecuador's upper crust, and I didn't have a thing to wear! Thankfully, my American friends in Quito were able to loan me a suit coat and tie, so at least I wouldn't be turned away by the palace guards due to inappropriate attire.

On the evening of the presentation ceremony, I took a taxi from my hotel to the Palacio Legislativo and was escorted into the hall where the ceremony would take place. I was seated in the balcony, among elegantly dressed señores and señoras of Ecuador's educated and wealthy class.

But soon after settling into my seat, I began to feel very, very ill. When the orchestra started to play the national anthem, conversation came to a quick halt and everyone—except for me—rose in unison as the president of Ecuador strode onto the stage. I was doubled over with abdominal pain and, despite the disgusted looks I was getting from my seatmates—who I suppose thought that the only American among them was making some sort of political statement—I just sat there and hoped that the pain would pass.

It eventually did, but by that time, everyone had taken their seats again, and the ceremony proceeded. I vaguely recall seeing Dr. Acosta-Solís cross the stage to shake hands with the president, but frankly, I was in so much pain—as one wave of cramps followed the next—that I didn't notice much of what was going on around me.

Following the ceremony, everyone else headed for the reception in another part of the building. But I walked as best I could and as quickly as possible to the nearest restroom where my bowels literally exploded. Once, twice, three times. I didn't know what was wrong, and of course I had no one to console me as I sat alone in the little cubicle, awaiting the next explosion. Exhausted, I was just sitting there, wondering what I could do, when I heard the restroom door open, and a worker—apparently believing that everyone had already gone home for the evening—turned off the lights! I said nothing, but just sat there in the dark, feeling so awful and so very lonely.

Eventually, the horror evidently over for the time being, I shuffled back and forth along the restroom wall until I found the light switch. Then I cleaned myself up and made my way back outside. But instead of taking a taxi back to my hotel, I thought it more prudent that I walk, in case I suddenly had to empty my bowels again. I chose a path across the huge, center-city El Hejido park where at one point, I did in fact have to duck behind a tree to throw up.

Back at the hotel, I ended up spending one of the worst nights of my life. Besides vomiting repeatedly into the waste can and dragging down the hall to a shared toilet to empty my bowels again and again, it turned out that *this* Hilton that I was staying in rented rooms "by the hour." So through the paper-thin walls, I had to listen to the sounds of panting and moaning and gasping couples as they passed the night away under completely different circumstances than my own.

The next several days were spent recovering to some degree, and I visited a medical center where I received a preliminary diagnosis of my condition: amoebic dysentery. I'd have to cut short my two-month trip and head back to Madison for treatment at the university's hospital.

During my stay in Ecuador, I had treated my drinking water with iodine— or just drank bottled Coca-Cola—and refrained from eating salads or raw vegetables, expressly to avoid exposing myself to harmful pathogens. But I let my guard down at least once, when a street vendor in a village outside of Portoviejo had offered me a "smoothie" of melon, shaved ice, and who-knows-what-else for free, just because I was a visiting American. I had wanted to refuse it, but that would have been a social gaffe not unlike the one I would later commit when I remained seated during the playing of the national anthem at the palace. As I drank the beverage, I recall my friend Fran looking at me wryly and saying, "Frozen amoebas, Whitey!" The way things turned out, she was probably right.

WHY THURSDAY?

FOR MORE THAN TWO DECADES NOW, I have set aside one day every week when I go alone to the woods to think-only-happy-thoughts and do no work. Many people know about my "second sabbath"—the other one being Sunday—but few people know why I chose *Thursday* in the first place.

I have often written the word Thursday in my daily journal as "Thor's Day," just for fun, in honor of the Norse god, Thor, from which the English word Thursday is derived. It wasn't until very recently, however, that I learned that the early Germanic tribes of northern Europe apparently set aside Thursday as a special day—in honor of their god of thunder and storms, Donar, the German equivalent of Thor—when they would go visit "the sacred groves" of trees! Perhaps, because half of my genes are German, I was genetically predisposed to choose Thursday for my *own* visits to the woods.

In fact, though, it was during the mid-1980s that I first began leaving town on a weekday to recharge my batteries. I'd never been fond of the cultural norm of five consecutive days of work—as I don't think anyone should have to spend that much of one's life working to meet basic needs—and I liked, too, the idea of having a day off when most everyone else was working.

At that time, I was teaching in the landscape program at Lane Community College, and all of my classes met on Mondays and Wednesdays. So those days were out. And Tuesday was not a good candidate, sandwiched as it was between two teaching days—as the "happy thoughts" on my day off were likely to be intruded upon by concerns about what I was going to be teaching the following day. Friday was simply too far from "mid-week" and too close to the weekend, so that was not a good choice. There was only one day left: Thursday.

Now that my Thursday tradition is nearly a quarter-century old, it's hard to imagine how life used to be when I stayed in town—and usually "worked" at least part of each day—for five or more consecutive days each week. And it is a rare Thursday, indeed, that I don't leave town these days. Of course, I occasionally end up missing a special speaker on campus or some other one-time event. But at such times, I simply wonder to myself, "Don't they know it's Thursday?"

Over the course of a typical year, my Thursday mini-vacations can add up to nearly fifty days away—or some seven weeks. That's even better than the generous vacation packages that "my people" back in Germany—as well as most other European workers—have come to expect, so I must be doing something right.

THE GEESE OF LATE APRIL

FIFTEEN YEARS AGO THIS WEEK, I spent the better part of a day here on the ridge lying on my back in a sunny clearing and watching flock after flock of geese fly overhead at a very high altitude and in a northwesterly direction. I'd noticed these geese other years, too, always toward the end of April, but never in such numbers. Because they fly so high as they cross the Cascades, I seldom see them at first, but rather *hear* them—and only very faintly at that. Thank goodness the only other audible sounds are typically just the wind and the occasional call of a raven, so that it's quiet enough to be *able* to hear their very faint calls.

For years, I wondered what kind of geese they were, why they flew so high, and where they were coming from and going to. But it didn't disturb me *not* to know. It was enough just to call them "late-April geese" and know that I could depend on hearing and seeing them every spring sometime toward the end of April.

Then, on 28 April 2009, I was driving up the heavily forested ridge here along the little paved forest road when, as I passed through a large clearing, a big, long-necked bird suddenly took flight quite near the road and flew parallel to my car for a hundred yards or more, right at eye-level, before heading up and over the trees. I got a very good look at the bird. It was a goose that was mostly gray in color except for a very noticeable patch of white on its forehead. When I returned to town later that day, I looked it up in my bird book and learned that it was a white-fronted (!) goose.

I have no idea, of course, how a solitary goose ended up in the roadside vegetation at the edge of a clearing in the otherwise densely forested West Cascades. But since I saw it at the end of April, I thought it had probably

97

become separated from its flock and had ended up landing in that very unlikely spot for a goose, far from any body of water.

Over the years, I have occasionally encountered other birds that were all alone and in areas that were completely inappropriate for them. None of the birds—including the goose I saw from the car—appeared to be injured; they were just "in the wrong place." My best guess is that the birds encountered a storm, were unable to continue in the direction they had been going, and out of sheer exhaustion were forced to land in a very unfamiliar and unsuitable place. There, they either died or, after a period of time, they recovered their strength and continued on.

At any rate, I was glad to be able to see what I presumed to be a "late-April goose" close enough to identify it, and to wish it well on its continued journey.

Today, my attention turned once again to the sky above me when I heard the faint calling of geese. Because it's partly cloudy—and the geese fly so high—I had an extraordinarily difficult time finding them. But at last, I caught a glimpse of a small skein of perhaps forty geese winging their way northwestward. As my "heart filled with gladness," I recalled the lovely poem by Edna St. Vincent Millay called *Wild Swans*:

> *I looked in my heart while the wild swans went over.*
> *And what did I see I had not seen before?*
> *Only a question less or a question more;*
> *Nothing to match the flight of wild birds flying.*
> *Tiresome heart, forever living and dying,*
> *House without air, I leave you and lock your door.*
> *Wild swans, come over the town, come over*
> *The town again, trailing your legs and crying!*

A STEADY STREAM OF VISITORS

O NE OF MY FAVORITE PASTIMES is to sit still somewhere for an hour or more—preferably far from other people and out-of-town—and just observe what other creatures are sharing that little piece of the planet with me that day. Earlier today, I returned to the ridge, where I plan to spend the next several days alone, just enjoying the peace-and-quiet and not having any commitments to keep.

When I arrived mid-morning at this clearing where I'd later be erecting my tent, I set up a little temporary kitchen at the base of a large, shrubby chinquapin, and began to prepare my breakfast. Before long, three dark-eyed juncos landed maybe twenty-five feet away from me and began feeding on moss sporophytes—the little hooded "capsules," borne at the tips of wiry stalks, in which mosses produce spores. The two birds with the darker-colored "hoods" were males, and the other a female. They've spent the winter at a lower elevation, and have just returned to the ridge, where they'll begin breeding in the next few weeks.

Over the course of the next hour, the juncos—always staying fairly close to one another—approached to within about six feet of me. These are not tame birds; they just sense no danger from me, as I'm sitting on the ground and, when I need to move, I do so slowly.

Meanwhile, I spied a chipmunk perhaps fifteen feet away. This little striped rodent probably spent the winter nearby, where it hibernated in a shallow burrow. With the return of spring and plenty to eat, the chipmunk is active again. Although it's likely never seen another human before, it too senses no danger from me, and allows me to walk within six or eight feet of it, as I move around the clearing now and again. I thought the chipmunk was eating grass stalks or perhaps last year's grass seed heads, but after a while, I realized that it, too, was eating moss sporophytes.

Suddenly, the juncos emitted a high-pitched squeak and headed for the bushes. And a fraction of a second later, the chipmunk that had appeared so nonchalant a moment before skittered to the edge of the clearing, to sit beneath a low-hanging fir branch. What had happened? When I glanced in the other direction, I caught just a glimpse of a sharp-shinned hawk as it sailed westward away from the clearing. The chipmunk evidently understood very well the juncos' alarm call!

A little later, I was startled by a tiny bird that dove right toward my red backpack. A hummingbird! Probably a rufous or an Anna's. This has happened many times before over the years. These energetic birds are especially drawn to red flowers, so perhaps they see my pack as a giant red flower full of nectar, but they seldom linger very long after discovering the hoax.

While eating my oatmeal, I heard a little cheep in the chinquapin behind me, and turned around to see what had made the noise. But I saw nothing, at least at first. Then I noticed a small branch quiver, as if a bird had just landed on it or taken off from it. I waited a few seconds until it revealed itself. It was a white-crowned sparrow, one of my favorite singers at this season! The top of its head is alternating stripes of white and beige, and its body is light brown. It wasn't in a singing mood at that moment, but I'm sure that I'll be hearing them in sunny clearings during the next few weeks.

During the comings and goings of the hummingbird and the sparrow, the juncos and the chipmunk continued their breakfasts only feet away from me. Soon, the hummingbird returned, but wasn't fooled this time by my pack; instead, it went directly to a manzanita shrub at the edge of the clearing, where I could see it nectaring on the just-opened little white flowers. Finally, while I was cleaning my breakfast dishes, a bumblebee flew slowly past me on its way to the manzanita flowers, as well.

Many naturalists actively seek particular birds or animals or flowers. But, for whatever reason, I'm a "passive" naturalist myself. I never go out to look for a particular bird, nor do I anticipate in advance what flowers might be in bloom when I go someplace. I don't pull apart rotten logs to look for salamanders, or turn over rocks in a stream in search of crayfish. It's so much more enjoyable and rewarding to just sit still and let the parade of visitors stream past me.

WATCHING BUD SCALES FALL EARTHWARD

HERE ON THE RIDGE, at an elevation of about 2,100 feet, it's about as idyllic a day as one could imagine: The temperature is 70 degrees; there's a nice up-ridge breeze from the west; the sun is shining; South Sister's snowy summit looms in the east; and there are no mosquitoes or other biting insects.

Although a casual visitor might not notice that anything is "going on" here—aside from the occasional passing fly or the sound of a hermit warbler singing in the treetops—"life" for all the ridge's plants and animals is in full swing. It's an especially big day for the Douglas-firs that comprise nearly one hundred percent of the forest's upper canopy.

So what's the big deal? Today is Bud-Break-Day for the firs as their tightly closed winter buds—which were formed early last summer—finally open up, permitting this year's needles and shoots to expand. As the buds open, they shed the papery scales called "bud scales" which then float away with the breeze. Sitting here in the under-canopy, I am mesmerized by the gentle rain of these bud scales and am reminded of their important role in the life of these giant Douglas-firs.

Every year, a tree grows bigger by adding a new length of shoot to the tip of all of its existing shoots (or "twigs") and another ring of wood around the perimeter of all of its existing shoots, branches, and trunks. And in preparation for the *next* year's shoot growth, most trees complete the formation of their buds encased in protective bud scales by early summer. Each bud—which contains all of the following year's leaves and flowers, but in miniature—then sits quietly at the tip of the new shoot for the rest of the summer, fall, and winter, and even for part of the spring.

Then, when conditions are just right, the bud opens and the miniaturized shoot begins to "extend" or grow. The bud scales, which are no longer useful, just fall or float to the ground. Things happen very fast at this point. From one day to the next, you can see or measure the increase in the length of the new shoot and the size of the new needles. And even though it's still only late spring or earliest summer, the new shoot soon forms the bud for the *following* year's shoot at its tip.

Think about that: Nearly a year in advance, all of the growth that will be added to the shoots in spring of 2012 is already in 2011 being planned for. And most of us think that humans are the only organism capable of planning ahead!

Let's review. Three very important annual events in the life of a tree occur in very rapid succession in spring: Bud break, shoot extension, and bud set. Boom-boom-boom! From start to finish, it takes just a matter of weeks for most temperate-zone trees to complete these three crucial tasks. Once shoot extension is complete and bud set has occurred, the tree settles down to photosynthesize for the rest of the summer, using the sugars produced in photosynthesis to add a new layer of wood to all of the existing shoots, branches, trunks, and roots. But that's another story for another time.

Meanwhile, the rain of bud scales continues here unabated, and all of those tiny, pre-formed needles that have been waiting in the darkness of the bud since early last summer, are finally getting a well-deserved breath of fresh air and a dose of sunlight, and life goes on. Just one more marvel in the fascinating world of trees.

FOOTPRINTS IN THE CATHEDRAL

O VER THE PAST 25 YEARS, I've gotten to know a square-mile patch of national forest land in the West Cascades quite well, having spent now nearly 700 days there. Even though the ridge is public land, I consider it to be sort of my private sanctuary, where no one else goes—unless invited by me.

The area is accessible by a paved forest road that leads to several wilderness trailheads farther up the ridge, and I occasionally encounter vehicles or people if I happen to be on or near the road. But it is rare indeed to meet someone out in The Woods itself. In fact, over all the years I've spent on the ridge, I've seen only *two* other people away from the road, and those two were on the same summer day more than ten years ago. And this is an area that is barely a mile from a major state highway!

Imagine my astonishment, then, to discover footprints one early-winter day in one of the most revered places in my sanctuary that I call The Cathedral. It is a stand of 400-plus-year-old Douglas-firs and equally ancient western red-cedars, through which the South Fork of my beloved Two Trout Creek flows. Most of the time, it is an intensely quiet place as it is shielded from highway noise by a shoulder of the ridge and a promontory called Little Smokey.

Over the years, only twice before have I seen evidence that someone else had visited The Cathedral, uninvited and unaccompanied by me. One time—during hunting season—I came upon a small pile of light blue toilet paper atop a large pile of human excrement. Another time, a hunter erected a portable "deer stand" in one of the younger redcedars near the west edge

103

of The Cathedral. Both of those discoveries were made several days or more after the visitor had been there.

But these footprints in the slushy snow on the forest floor were fresh. Wet snow had fallen overnight and covered the ground to a depth of a couple of inches. And although the snow had already stopped falling several hours earlier, that which remained in the upper canopy was now dropping to the ground as daytime temperatures climbed toward the forties, so any footprints were being quickly covered with snow falling from the treetops.

I placed my size nine boot next to one of the prints. It was almost exactly the same size. Although hunting season was over, it was possible that someone had not been able to "get his deer" during the legal season, and was now taking advantage of the first snow to more easily find his quarry. (Poaching is a widespread problem and under-reported crime on public land.)

Because my Thursdays in the woods are reserved for what I call "happy thoughts," I tried not to think about possible poaching. Instead, I focused on following the tracks to see where they might lead. They came down—or perhaps went up—the slope south of the creek; I couldn't tell which direction they were headed due to their blurriness in the slushy snow.

I decided to take a chance that the person had come *down* the slope from the ridge, so I followed the tracks in the other direction, out of The Cathedral and into a clearing where they were more distinct, since there was no forest canopy there to drop melting snow onto them and blur them. After a dozen yards or so, I realized that these were not boot prints after all. They looked instead like the tracks of someone with huge feet who was walking *barefoot* in the snow. Then I noticed five deep holes in the snow at the front of each print. Claw marks. Aha! I wasn't following someone who was barefoot, after all; these were *bear* footprints.

What a relief! Although I don't like to find evidence that other human beings have visited my sanctuary, I am happy to know that the occasional bear saunters through the area, even if it does leave tracks on the otherwise pristine floor of The Cathedral.

EUGENE'S SUMMER WEATHER:
BEST IN THE U.S.?

MOST AMERICANS SPEND FAR MORE TIME OUTSIDE during the three months of summer than they do during the other nine months put together. But summertime fun in many parts of the country involves at least one drawback such as biting insects, high humidity, uncomfortably high temperatures, or summer rainstorms that often include lightning. Here in Eugene, however, at the south end of the Willamette Valley in western Oregon, almost every day between mid-June and mid-September is close to perfect for being outside.

TEMPERATURE: Although separated from the Pacific Ocean by the Coast Range of mountains, the cold water off the coast of Oregon helps to keep daytime temperatures moderate. The average daily high in both July and August is around 82 degrees. (The record high for Eugene is 108 degrees on both 9 and 10 August 1981.) And in a typical summer, the daily high exceeds 90 degrees on only fifteen days.

But it's at night that the weather is truly refreshing. While most places east of the Great Plains remain quite warm during summer nights—due to humid air's ability to retain more heat than dry air—Eugene's clear skies and low humidity combine to produce very comfortable nights. The average nightly low in both July and August is a pleasant 51 degrees. There are many summer days when the difference between the daytime high and the nighttime low exceeds thirty degrees, and some when it exceeds forty.

Other cities in the West may offer some or many of the other attributes listed below, but temperatures are not as comfortable as in Eugene. For example, Seattle, Washington, and Vancouver, British Columbia, because of their proximity to Puget Sound, don't get as warm during the day, nor as cool at night as Eugene. And cities farther south—e.g., Medford, Oregon and Sacramento, California—get uncomfortably hot on many days and remain quite warm overnight.

PRECIPITATION: Like most West Coast cities, Eugene has a winter-wet/summer-dry or "Mediterranean" climate. Annual precipitation is about fifty inches—only slightly more than the typical Midwestern or Mid-Atlantic city—but 80 percent of that falls between November and April. The summer months are especially dry, with July and August averaging less than an inch of rain each month, and even June and September averaging only about an inch and a half per month.

In cities east of the Great Plains, on the other hand, about the same amount of precipitation—three to four inches—falls during every month of the year, so summers are just as wet most years as the other seasons are.

HUMIDITY: Although the air in much of the West has relatively low humidity in the summer, the converse is true for anywhere east of the Great Plains, where the high humidity can be truly suffocating. In Eugene, the *average* relative humidity at 4 p.m. during the months of July and August is just under 40 percent.

Another benefit of the low humidity is the clarity of the air. Areas of the U.S. with high relative humidity in the summer have many hazy days with whitish skies that create glare and visual discomfort. Eugene's skies, on the other hand, are almost always a deep blue—despite occasional light haze due to dust and pollen that sometimes accumulate in the absence of air-cleansing summer rainfall. But such conditions seldom persist for long, and disappear once fresh air blows in again from the Pacific.

SUNSHINE: Few meteorological conditions have such a positive influence on attitude as sunny skies do. And because Eugene has a relatively sunless winter—with an average of twenty-five partly-cloudy or cloudy days per month in both December and January—the sun is an especially welcome sight, once it arrives. Although some days, especially in early summer, may begin with "morning clouds," these clouds typically dissipate by mid- to late-forenoon. On average, July has 24 sunny or partly sunny days and August has 23.

SEVERE STORMS: Although afternoon and evening thunderstorms often develop during the summer in the Cascade Mountains east of Eugene, they seldom spill over to the Willamette Valley. In a typical year, lightning occurs in the *greater* Eugene area on fewer than five days—and in Eugene itself, on only one or two days. Tornadoes have occasionally touched down in the southern Willamette Valley, but they are very rare and always small. And hurricanes are simply unheard of in this region.

INSECTS: In much of the U.S.—especially, again, east of the Great Plains—one's outdoor experiences in the summertime are greatly limited or at least compromised by an abundance of biting insects. Parts of the U.S. suffer from black flies, deer flies, and other biting insects, in addition to mosquitoes. But because of Eugene's dry summer and the lack of lakes and ponds, mosquitoes are few in number and tend to be confined to neighborhoods in the vicinity of the Willamette River, which runs through the city. But even there, the mosquitoes are generally a nuisance only during a brief period in late evening, due to our windy days—during which mosquitoes lie low—and our cool nights, during which most mosquitoes are inactive.

ALLERGIES: During parts of May and June, Eugene has some of the highest pollen counts in the nation. That's because the city is located south of more than 300,000 acres of grass-seed fields, and the prevailing north wind in late spring blows all that grass pollen into the city. But high grass pollen counts last only a few weeks, and the rest of the summer is largely free of allergy-causing pollens. In other parts of the U.S., this is seldom the case, where a variety of weeds with allergy-causing pollen (e.g., ragweed) release their pollen throughout the summer.

BREEZINESS: Even though some other parts of the U.S. (especially in the West) may have many or even all of the attributes listed above that Eugene has, they typically lack a very important contributor to comfort when outdoors in the summer, and that is air movement. Once again, Eugeneans have it made: On an almost daily basis, from May until September, the day dawns with still air, but by mid- to late-morning, a north breeze—or, rather, a *wind*—picks up and continues most days until sunset. Even on very hot days, when the temperature is in the 90s, it is comfortable to be outside, especially if one is in the shade, as the constant air movement has a very pleasant cooling effect.

Interestingly, the town of Corvallis—located just forty miles north-northwest of Eugene, at the foot of the Coast Range, and with a climate very similar to that of Eugene—does *not* generally have the daily north wind, so it can really sizzle on unusually hot summer days. However, the relatively still air during the heat of the day is compensated for by the glorious sea breeze that arrives in Corvallis around 4:30 p.m. on an almost daily basis in the summer, bringing cool air in from the west and dropping the temperature from the 90s or 80s into the very comfortable 70s by dinnertime. Eugene, on the other hand, lies farther out into the Willamette Valley, and benefits less frequently from these cool evening breezes which often dissipate before they reach Eugene.

Although it may not be the best summer climate for growing tomatoes and melons—because of the cool nights—it's a nearly perfect climate for making human beings happy. You should see the smiles on the faces of Eugene residents every year once summer arrives on the heels of our usual cool and damp spring!

(This essay appeared in the Commentary *section of Eugene, Oregon's* Register-Guard *newspaper on Sunday, 28 July 2013.)*

AUTUMN IN AUGUST

ALTHOUGH I ENJOY EVERY SEASON of the year, I have to admit a special affinity for fall—or "autumn," as the more poetic among us refer to it. Thankfully, it comes only once a year, so I don't risk taking the season for granted.

To most people, fall means shorter and cooler days and a sun that is lower in the sky than it was all summer. And here in the middle latitudes, it means the time of year when the leaves of deciduous trees and shrubs acquire their so-called fall colors just before they drop.

But one tree here in western Oregon goes through its annual "autumn" ritual in the middle of the summer! That tree is the Pacific madrone (*Arbutus menziesii*), a broad-leafed tree that is evergreen. *All* evergreen trees—be they broad-leafed or needle-leafed ("conifers")—lose *some* of their oldest leaves every year and at a particular season during the year. For madrones, that season is now.

The past few weeks, each time I've visited the madrone stands here on the ridge, I've noticed that their leaves produced in 2010 have been drooping more and more, turning yellow, and falling off. The new leaves that they produced this year (2011) are now fully developed, so there is apparently no longer any need for last year's leaves, and off they come.

It happens slowly at first, but this week, the ground beneath the madrones is covered with new-fallen leaves in various stages of drying out and turning from gold to brown. A few of 2010's leaves still remain on the trees, but they're sure to fall within the next week or so. Walking through the madrone groves—which was a mostly quiet experience only a few weeks ago—is now quite a noisy endeavor, as the fallen, drying leaves quickly acquire a crispness so that footsteps atop them produce a very audible "crunch."

The mid-summer leaf-fall of madrones is lovely enough, but these wondrous trees shed something else at this season: their bark! Madrones are almost universally adored for the smooth, pink or red bark that develops on their trunks and branches. And the *outer* layer of madrone bark is shed every year at about the same time as the older leaves are dropping.

The shedding of the bark begins when the outermost layer of bark splits open, usually in a longitudinal direction, and over the next few days, it peels back in pieces of varying sizes, depending on the size of the branch or trunk. Small branches lose pieces of bark that are just a fraction of a square inch, but larger trunks can shed their bark in sheets the size and feel of pieces of paper. With each gust of wind, another piece or two of bark breaks off from the trunk and falls to the ground. The larger pieces become "unique" writing paper for nature-boys like me. I love writing little notes on madrone bark and sending them to friends, especially those who do not live within the natural range of madrones—which is from southern Vancouver Island to Baja California, always west of the Cascade-Sierra axis.

The new bark underneath that which is shed has, at first, a light beige color. But over the next weeks and months, it will acquire the more familiar pink or red color that one associates with these trees. Unlike most other trees in the maritime Pacific Northwest, madrones have few epiphytes (mosses, lichens, and ferns) growing on their branches and trunks because the epiphytes would of course be shed along with the outer layer of bark every summer.

I realize that, to some people, the madrones look as if they are dying right now. Many of their leaves have turned yellow and are falling off, and their bark is splitting open and hanging briefly in shreds on the branches and trunks before falling to the ground. But the madrones know what they're doing. They're providing dendrophiles like me with a mid-summer spectacle—that truly rivals the finest October display of any deciduous broad-leafed tree—when both their old leaves and their old bark fall off simultaneously. And because no other trees are "performing" at the same time, the madrones benefit from *all* of my attention—instead of having to share it with countless other species of trees, as they would in mid-October!

COUNTING MY BLESSINGS

IT'S THE FRIDAY AFTER THANKSGIVING and I'm here in the West Cascades, sitting shirtless in a sun-drenched stand of young conifers. Over my right shoulder, I have a splendid view to the snow-covered ridge-top on the other side of the McKenzie River valley. Air temperature is in the mid-40s and there's only a very slight breeze. Even the occasional flies that visit me seem less annoying today than usual, spending the bulk of their time atop nearby sunlit logs, basking, just like me.

What a great day to be alive! Other than the occasional call of a winter wren or a red-breasted nuthatch, and the distant sound of the rushing McKenzie River a mile or so away, it is absolutely quiet. I'm certainly having a very different day compared to many other Americans on this Black Friday, traditionally the biggest shopping day of the year.

As I near the end of my sixth decade on the planet, I'm reminded of how pleasant my life truly is. That's one of the reasons I've come to the woods for three days over this Thanksgiving weekend: to simply reflect on all I have to be thankful for.

I'm most thankful for my health, both physical and (apparently) mental. I have no chronic aches or pains, despite my advancing age. My five senses all remain top-notch and I've experienced no hearing loss or any significant changes in my vision.

In addition to a decent set of genes and some darn good luck, I suspect that the lifestyle I have chosen is responsible, at least in part, for my health. To help ensure my continued physical health, I get places under my own power, mostly by bicycle; I've never owned a car. Plus, I swim laps three days a week at the pool and almost daily work outside, at least a little bit, in the garden or at one of my community landscape projects. To help maintain my mental health, I live a life unencumbered by "things" and the often accompanying fear that someone might take some of them from me. And some fifty or sixty days every year—one day a week, at the very least—I get away to the woods just to enjoy the peace and quiet, and to "recharge my batteries."

I am fortunate, too, to live in a community that places a high value on its parks, natural areas, and public transit system, and that is bicycle-friendly. It is because of these amenities—all of which are important to my well-being—that I chose to live in Eugene in the first place, back in 1983. I appreciate, as well, the access I have in Eugene to so-called natural foods stores and to the university's facilities, especially the libraries.

I'm also grateful to be able to do only the work I want to do, and when and how I want to do it. I am nobody's 40-hour-a-week slave. Granted, I lack the high income and many benefits that such jobs usually provide, but in exchange, I have a "life" that I savor every day of the week that most workers—whether white- or blue-collared—don't generally get to enjoy except on weekends, holidays, and after retirement, if they live that long.

Financially, I am quite well-off, considering I typically earn less than $10,000 per year. I was able to buy my little 528-square-foot house at a fairly young age, so I have no monthly mortgage payments. And, other than expenditures for food and limited home improvements and taxes, I spend very little money—no car, no expensive hobbies or fancy clothes, no kids in college, no health insurance. So, despite my comparatively low income, I've been able over the years to put away a substantial sum of money that could help with an emergency expense or simply supplement my social security income if I ever choose to retire.

I am thankful, too, that I have many friends in my community who support me in a variety of ways and appreciate the work that I do—and who, were I in need of something, would likely come to my aid. I don't *expect* that response from anyone, but I'm confident of it, based on past experience.

Not least of all, I am grateful to have back in Eugene a roof over my head when I need it and three very valuable appliances: a natural-gas stove for heat, a refrigerator-freezer, and a stovetop-oven. These are all luxuries that not everyone in the world has, and I remind myself regularly of how truly privileged I am to be able to afford and enjoy these attributes of civilization.

Now it's time for me to return to the tasks at hand: enjoying the solitude and the quiet of this lovely spot, basking in the day's remaining sunshine, and counting, then re-counting, my many, many blessings.

RIVERSIDE OR RIDGETOP?
WHICH WILL IT BE?

DURING THE EARLY YEARS of my weekly trips to the woods, I spent most of my time along rivers or creeks. I was naturally drawn to them—as are most humans—and especially appreciated the way the rushing water largely muffled all other sounds, from buzzing insects to aircraft flying overhead. After all, I was looking for some peace-and-quiet (or P&Q), having spent the preceding six days in Eugene.

If the weather was hot, there was usually a nice pool nearby to jump into. If there were a few mosquitoes, I could sit on a mossy boulder in the creek's shallows, where the inevitable up-canyon breeze would keep the insects away. And there was often something of special interest to observe—a family of harlequin ducks might float by or, occasionally, I would see a mink or an otter.

In winter, when many days here in the West Cascades are sunny, it became a little trickier to find warm, sunny creek-side spots when the sun was so low in the sky that many valley-bottom areas were in the shadow of a nearby ridge for weeks, even months, at a time. But I quickly learned to avoid those areas and seek out the places where, even at the winter solstice in late December, the sun would peek over the ridge and warm me at my creek-side day-nest.

Over the years, however, I began to spend more and more time here on the ridge, and I came to appreciate my P&Q days here even more than those spent next to moving water. One needs to understand, though, that I am not referring to a knife-edge ridge where one can see down both sides of the ridge to the creeks in the adjacent canyon-bottoms—and hear those creeks, too. The ridge where I now spend so many of my precious days away from town is very broad and nearly flat, with steep drop-offs on both sides to the adjacent valleys or canyons. It is an ancient intra-canyon lava flow that, in the area I frequent most, is nearly a mile across. That means that most of the ridge is acoustically protected from sounds in the adjacent valleys, be they the sounds of moving water or of traffic—as one of the valleys contains a busy state highway.

It is true that, here on the ridgetop, I sometimes hear the aircraft and other unwanted sounds which in the adjacent valley bottoms were inaudible or largely muffled by the sound of fast-moving water. But when those sounds are absent—which they are for much of the time—then I get to hear pure, undistilled q – u – i – e – t , which is an absolute treat.

And if I need water to drink or want to go for a dip on a hot summer day, there is a small creek right here on the ridge that meets those needs, so I don't have to descend into one of the "noisy" valleys to refresh myself.

I suppose another drawback of the ridgetop is that, at night, I can hear from my tent "cracking sticks" in the event that a large animal is making its way through the forest—or toward my tent—whereas I was usually pleasantly ignorant of the presence of large animals when I camped near noisy creeks. On the other hand, hearing "cracking sticks" can alert me to potential danger, and it is in fact a rare night when I do hear such sounds.

As I have become more aware of and appreciative of natural silence here on the ridge, it has made my return to the noise of the city more difficult. But I'm happy to have rediscovered something that our ancestors likely took for granted: the importance of natural silence and the need to occasionally leave behind the sounds—including that of running water—that prevent us from experiencing genuine peace-and-quiet.

How could I have known in my younger years that, by spending so much time near moving water, I was muffling not only the unwanted sounds of, say, distant chainsaws and aircraft, but the sound of silence, too?

A MEANING-FILLED EXCHANGE
OF VERY FEW WORDS

WHILE WAITING IN LINE at a downtown Eugene natural foods store, I noticed a young man two check-stands away who looked familiar to me, and I wondered if maybe he had been one of my university students a few years earlier. When he briefly glanced in my direction, I smiled and nodded—but he didn't acknowledge me, or maybe just didn't notice. And because of my uncertainty about his identity, I made no more effort to get his attention.

A few minutes later, while loading my groceries into my bicycle baskets just outside the store's front door, I noticed him again, standing at the other end of the bike rack and using his phone. Suddenly, he interrupted his conversation briefly and said, "Whitey!" I looked up at him, convinced now that we did in fact know each other, and signaled to him that I'd left something inside the store, and would come over to say hello when I returned.

When I got closer, I realized that it was Ned, who'd been in my Trees Across Oregon class in spring 2007. He was one of my favorite students that term, so full of youthful energy, confident of himself, and very comfortable around the other students and around me. He was still on his phone, but I went up to him and gave him a hug. We smiled at each other, but he was clearly very distracted by his telephone conversation, so I nodded goodbye and went to unlock my bicycle and pedal home to lunch.

When I looked over at him one more time before I left, he caught my glance and shouted, "You changed my life—best class I ever took!" I smiled at him again before crossing the street, but he was already back on his phone.

The whole way home, I couldn't stop thinking about our chance meeting. We hadn't seen each other in nearly three years—since he handed in his final exam in early June 2007—and our "conversation" was extremely brief. In fact, I don't recall saying a single word to him the whole time, and all he said was my name, and then his parting comment. But the few words he did say really stayed with me.

I have no idea whatsoever how Ned's life changed as the result of taking my class and getting to know me. Nor will he ever have any idea how his comment affected me. The chances of our ever meeting again are slim indeed. He took my class as a freshman and is presumably a senior by now, and nearly ready to graduate and leave Eugene.

Our brief encounter made me reflect on how each of us affects the lives of others in myriad and mysterious ways. Ned was not one of my better students academically, but he evidently got something from my class even more important than a good grade—something that gave his life a new direction and purpose, and for which he is grateful.

And I was reminded that my success as a teacher can sometimes be measured in ways other than the grades my students receive at the end of the course.

A VERY TINY SIP OF WATER

O N AN UNUSUALLY HOT AFTERNOON in early September—with noisy construction work going on next door—I decided to get out of the house and find someplace cool and quiet where I could relax. One option was to bike down to the beautiful Willamette River that flows through the middle of Eugene. But another possibility was to head to campus, which was almost empty during intersession, and dangle my feet in the cool water of a quiet courtyard fountain near Cascade Hall. I chose the latter.

It was late enough in the afternoon that the courtyard was already in the shade, which made it even more pleasant. I sat down beside the little pool at the base of the cascading water, took off my sandals, and put my feet and lower legs into the cool water. It was refreshing, indeed. After five or ten minutes, I lifted my wet legs back onto the pool's concrete edge and proceeded to edit a report that I had been working on at my home office.

Although campus was nearly deserted, I was soon joined at the fountain by another visitor seeking respite from the hot afternoon. I had my head in my papers when I felt something on one of the toes. I thought a fly had landed on me, so I twitched my toes and it went away. A few seconds later, it returned to the very same toe, and this time I looked up to see that my little visitor was not a fly after all, but a yellow-jacket.

When "confronted" with yellow-jackets, most people in our culture respond by shooing the insects away—and maybe screaming at the same time. But I learned long ago that such behavior was unnecessary, and in fact could result in an unwanted sting. After all, the yellow-jackets we see flying around during the summer are usually solitary female workers—like honey bees—who are just doing their jobs, whether that is to bring food back to the colony or shredded-up wood to turn into "paper" and add to the growing nest. These insects don't want anything from us—unless, of course, we're eating a peanut-butter-and-jelly sandwich, or holding in our hands a piece of barbecued chicken. Even then, though, they mean no harm. All they want is for us to share with them a bit of our food—a very, very *tiny* bit.

So I watched the yellow-jacket with interest. She was a welcome distraction from my work. As she moved back and forth across the tender skin of my toe, it created such a tickling sensation that I was really tempted to wiggle my toes and chase her away, even though I knew she would do me no harm.

The yellow-jacket continued to sit on my toe, but she was not resting. She was clearly intent on something, but I wasn't quite sure what. Then I saw what she was finding so attractive and worth her prolonged visit. At the base of my toenail was a tiny drop of water, all that remained on my feet from their earlier dip in the pool. That tiny drop was the yellow-jacket's equivalent of the courtyard pool to which I'd come to refresh myself. There she stood, at the edge of her little private drop of water, lapping it up and refreshing herself on a hot day, before flying home for the evening.

A few minutes later, after she'd departed, I packed my satchel, hopped on my bike, and flew back to my own home for dinner, content to have shared part of the hot afternoon with one of nature's hard-working hexapods.

A FAIRY IN THE BAY OF THE ANGELS

(This essay was initially written in March 1993—well before I began essay-writing in earnest in 2004—and was then revised slightly in 2011.)

ONE OF OUR CAMPSITES during this year's field class to Baja California in mid-March was by the stunningly beautiful and remote Bahía de los Angeles (Bay of the Angels) on the east side of the peninsula. We had a grand view out across the tranquil, sapphire bay to the enormous Isla del Angel de la Guarda (Guardian Angel Island) that "guards" the bay's entrance. During the day, tropical frigatebirds flew overhead, and an on-shore breeze kept the camp from getting too hot. In the evening, we were treated to distant guitar music and singing by a half-dozen Mexican men who worked all day at a tiny fish processing plant a quarter of a mile from our camp, and then enjoyed making a little music together before heading home to their families in the small village another mile or so down the beach.

But it was the night life along the bay that was really remarkable. Both of the nights that we spent at the isolated site were moonless, so the sky was simply filled with stars. The first night, I accompanied several of my students down to the shore after dark. As the day's wind had by then died down, the surface of the bay was almost completely still; the only sound we could hear was the gentle lapping of miniature waves breaking along the sandy beach. Upon closer inspection, we noticed that every time a wavelet broke, the water lit up as if filled with tiny lights. Some of us had heard about the occasional appearance of bioluminescent microörganisms or "tiny glowing creatures" in tropical waters, but this was the first time any of us had seen such a spectacle. It was enchanting to watch, and we were soon

120

splashing our hands in the water and watching it light up in response, as any slight disturbance of the water made the critters glow briefly.

We walked back to camp, grinning from our new experience and looking forward to yet another rest-filled Baja night, with the absolute stillness punctuated only now and again by the yapping of coyotes in the surrounding hills.

The next night, after darkness had fallen, the entire class descended to the edge of the bay, as some of the students had missed the show the night before and we were hoping for a repeat performance. We were not disappointed. Conditions were almost identical to the previous night, and we spent much time playing along the beach, splashing in the wavelets and throwing sand and pebbles into the water to watch the light show that resulted from it.

I don't know quite what came over me—and why I hadn't thought of doing this before—but without saying a word to anyone else, I began to remove my clothes, after which I proceeded into the water. With every step I took away from the shore, the water surrounding my foot and leg would light up for an inch or so in every direction. My students and I were enraptured, and the whispered sounds of "Wow!" and "Amazing!" were all that broke the otherwise still air.

About twenty feet from the shore—where the ten students were lined up for an "aerial view" (relatively speaking) of my nocturnal excursion into the bay—the water was deep enough for me to stoop down and immerse myself up to my neck. I then gently and quietly pushed forward into the water, paralleling the shoreline, and began to slowly swim the breaststroke in the warm water. When I first pushed my hands out in front of me, I watched as countless little lights flowed around my fingers, down along my forearms, and then disappeared under my chin. The "ooo's" and "ahhh's" from the class were non-stop. From their vantage point, not only was my entire body outlined in soft light as I moved through the otherwise pitch-black water, but in my wake the gently churned water looked as if glowing glitter was being shed from my body into the sea.

Soon, several of my students had quietly disrobed and joined me in the water. As we giggled together in utter delight, we subconsciously muted our voices as if fearing that loud sounds would destroy the magic we were witnessing. As I swam slowly back and forth and repeatedly rolled over on my back to watch the light-filled water trail away behind my legs, I was reminded of the old Walt Disney television shows introduced by an animated Tinkerbelle, fairy wand in hand, who floated onto the screen all a-twinkle and followed by a trail of sparkle. I thought to myself, "So *this* is what it must be like to be a fairy!" and broke into a smile as wide as the star-filled sky.

ABOUT THE AUTHOR

Born and reared in Pennsylvania—first in Jersey Shore, a small town in the mountains of the north-central part of the state, and later in Lancaster in the southeastern part of the state—Whitey Lueck left the U.S. in 1974 after graduating with a degree in horticulture from Pennsylvania State University. In northern Sweden, he spent the summer milking cows on a small farm and picking berries in the surrounding forests. He then interned as a horticulturist and landscape designer for municipal parks departments in Nantes, France, and in Bern, Switzerland, before returning to the U.S. in 1977 to pursue a graduate degree in forest ecology at Oregon State University in Corvallis. He has lived in western Oregon ever since, except for a two-year hiatus at the University of Wisconsin in Madison.

A popular speaker and the author of countless articles about trees and what he calls "the world around us," Whitey began formally writing essays in 2004. His first collection of essays—published in 2015 and called *Staying Put in Lane County*—recounted his activities and musings during the 2014 calendar year when he purposely never left his home county. And his second collection of essays—called *Words from the Woods: 2004-2008*—was published in 2016.

Whitey teaches part-time at the University of Oregon in the Department of Landscape Architecture, and lives not far from campus on a very nature-friendly property that has a front *woodland* instead of a front *lawn*. The entire property is open to the public, with appropriate signage that explains different aspects of the site. The relatively small residential lot showcases a household that produces all of its own fruits and vegetables (as well as eggs and honey), makes its own electricity (from rooftop solar panels), and has neither a garage nor a driveway (because Whitey has never owned a car).